ORGANIC
GARDENING

An unsprayed garden full of flowers, shrubs and trees will be a haven for insects, birds and other wild life.

ORGANIC GARDENING

Ann Bonar

WARD LOCK

ACKNOWLEDGEMENTS

The publishers gratefully acknowledge the following agencies and photographer for granting permission to reproduce the colour photographs: Harry Smith Horticultural Photographic Collection (pp. 2, 11, 18, 27, 31, 39, 46, 47 & 62); Pat Brindley (pp. 15 & 55); Photos Horticultural Picture Library (pp. 23 & 87); and Ann Bonar (pp. 58 & 67).

All the line drawings are by Nils Solberg.

The quotations on p. 8 are from *The Gardener's Year* by Karl Capek, published by George Allen & Unwin, 1929, and are reproduced by kind permission of Unwin Hyman Ltd.

First published in Great Britain in 1990
by Ward Lock Limited, Artillery House,
Artillery Row, London SW1P 1RT,
a Cassell Company

House editor Denis Ingram
Designed by Anita Ruddell

Text filmset in Bembo
by Hourds Typographica, Stafford
Printed and bound in Portugal
by Resopal

**British Library Cataloguing in Publication
Data**

Bonar, Ann
   Organic gardening,
   1. Gardens, Organic cultivation
   I. Title   II. Series
   635.0484

ISBN 0 7063 6873 8

CONTENTS

INTRODUCTION

Gardening the organic way could be said to be the lazy man's way of gardening – leave the plants to their own devices, don't spray anything and let the balance of Nature take over. Unfortunately, if you do that, the result is likely to be a garden full of the more rampant wild plants, usually called weeds.

Gardening organically is more a way of growing the plants you want specifically in the garden, and giving them as much help as you can to grow strong and healthy, but without using what are termed 'chemical' pesticides, weedkillers or fertilizers. Gardening like this is creative. A community of plants, insects, birds, frogs and all the other many living inhabitants of the garden, is built up with checks and balances within it which prevent any one species dominating another. The gardener chooses the plants which are to grow there, uses a variety of cultivation techniques to maintain them, and sprays or fertilizes only with harmless materials which occur naturally, and only when absolutely essential.

If you introduce into this balanced equilibrium an alien substance which kills one particular species completely, it is obvious that the whole life structure is disrupted, not simply one kind of insect or fungus. It can take them months, if not years, to recreate and restore a working, harmonious collection of living creatures.

However, it is worth remembering that this is not necessarily harmonious in the sense that everything in it is living at peace with its neighbours; jungle warfare still exists, 'dog eats dog', and indeed has to, in order that the desired balance can be maintained. It is no good being squeamish about the species of slugs which cannabilize other slugs, if you want to grow lettuce without resorting to metaldehyde. But the cannibal slugs themselves will be kept in check, perhaps by beetles, perhaps by frogs or hedgehogs and, as the area is a garden, by the organic gardener during night-time hunting.

Those who are new to any kind of gardening or who already garden conventionally, and who would like to garden organically, might well say that gardening is organic anyway, as it deals with living things. But the crucial difference between the two lies mainly in the use of chemicals to kill pests, and in the use of concentrated powder or granular fertilizers synthesized from the by-products of manufacturing.

The inorganic gardener will attack at once with chemical solutions which have an overkill effect, as well as destroying any predators or parasites which would do the job just as well, and for free. Weeds will be eliminated with a blanket spray or powder which will also eradicate what might have been choice new seedling hybrids from cultivated plants, and it can affect the soil inhabitants, too. Plant foods will be supplied by concentrated fertilizers (to boost the food content of the soil) which provide an almost instant but short-lived improvement, but do not sustain the soil structure; with its deterioration plants deteriorate too. The structure of the soil – the way the soil particles are held together – becomes poor, so that plants are unable to develop good root systems, and hence good top growth. Consequently the plant cannot absorb the food it needs through its roots, the fertilizer builds up in the soil, and even more trouble ensues.

The use of chemicals as described is a quick, easy way to deal with trouble, but it is another expression of the tendency to deal with the symptoms rather than the cause, and the cause can be traced back to either a beginning which was wrong, or to a cultural technique used when the plant was established, which was not suited to it or was wrongly performed.

The organic gardener substitutes good growing methods, what used to be called good husbandry, for chemicals. Much, much more attention is paid to the plant and its individual needs, so that these can be met and catered for. All this takes more time, naturally, and perhaps this is where the moment of truth comes for many of you.

Gardening is a hobby; hobbies are undertaken because they are pleasurable, and there is no pleasure in pursuing a hobby if it is done badly and, in the case of gardening, the end product is a sick, ugly, stunted plant. It will always take more time to do a job properly, to grow a strong resistant plant, rather than just press a knob for an instant blast of vaporizer, like a space invader. Giving time to a hobby is a measure of one's enthusiasm, and an indication of one's priorities.

EFFECT ON ENVIRONMENT

There is another, more significant, side to organic gardening with much wider implications. Owning a piece of land at all is a privilege; to have somewhere to grow food of one's own was an immense step forward for the mediaeval peasant, but with the increasingly sophisticated organization of society, food became easily available from other sources than one's own soil and labour.

The field became the garden, a place of ornament rather than utility, particularly when the flow of new plants from other countries turned from a trickle into a flood. Cultivating these new plants took skill and knowledge, and so growing plants on one's land became a hobby. We may think we are poor, but most people that want to, own a piece of soil; in mediaeval times the reverse was the case – only the rich owned land – and because there is now so much land used as gardens in the hands of so many people, the total area now has a considerable impact on the environment in general.

Wherever a garden is, whether it is in a town centre, in the suburbs, or in the remotest countryside, what you do to it will have an effect on its surroundings in some way. If you keep drenching it with chemical solutions and upsetting the fine balance referred to earlier, the consequences will literally seep out into the soil and the air outside the garden, and add to the pollutants already present. You will affect birds, animals, other insects, outside your own garden, and ultimately, albeit indirectly, other people.

Owning a garden is, like all other privileges, a responsibility too; owning even just one houseplant means owning an embryonic garden, and there is no excuse for zapping the greenfly, when removing it by hand would do the trick just as well – better still, grow the plant in the right place from the start. If you grow the plants in your garden with sympathy and awareness of what they require for good health, you will not need to resort to blunt implements to cure the sickness that comes to them from your lack of understanding.

You will also be having an effect on the future environment by your treatment of your garden. Caring for it organically will ultimately result in 'cleaner' air and soil outside it, as well as in it, and make it easier for the gardening generations who come after you. Because of course they always will – gardening is, after all, not 'a bucolic and meditative occupation. It is an insatiable passion', for which 'the gardener wants (a lifetime of) eleven hundred years' – less is not long enough.

Chapter 1

The Unsprayed Garden

A garden contains a mixture of different kinds of plants: trees, shrubs, grass, roses, flowering plants in herbaceous borders, water plants if you have a pond, mountain plants if you have a rock garden, and so on. Within all these different groups, there are hundreds and hundreds of varieties that could be grown, and the ones that are, depend on your choice and needs. Each garden is therefore literally a unique collection of plants, unlike any other. As it grows and is assembled, it develops its own ecology, its own balance of Nature in which its inhabitants are inextricably reliant on one another.

HABITATS

In every garden there are definite areas which evolve either by intention or of their own accord, which make up a particular habitat. A pond is an obvious example, with its floating water plants, submerged plants and marginal species, its snails, fish, newts and frogs, dragonflies and water-beetles. Another is a rock garden, whose plants require a specialized environment of quite a different kind; unfortunately, the main animal inhabitants here are all too often slugs and snails.

One area might be shaded by trees so that some of the soil is in deep shade, and some has a mixture of sunlight and shade as the sun shines through gaps in the trees' canopy. This will eventually contain woodland varieties of plants and animals, such as birds nesting in the trees, perching on them before going on to other parts of the garden, bees swarming, flies, caterpillars, moths, squirrels; whatever they are, they are all creatures of woodland habitats needing trees and the shade beneath them. All combine to live together without dominating one another.

A garden which has an area of soil which lets moisture pass through it rapidly, at the same time faces south and is sheltered from strong wind, also dictates the growing of a particular type of plant, i.e., that which is suited to Mediterranean conditions. There is therefore yet another collection of insects, fungi, and animals which again build up their own state of equilibrium, different from all the others, but nevertheless still broadly dependent on them.

VARIETY IN THE GARDEN

From this it can be seen that an unsprayed garden is a fascinating and incredibly mixed collection of forms of life – you could find a green woodpecker in the woodland, starlings on the lawn, leafhoppers on the roses(!), tadpoles in the pool and strawberry snails in the rock-garden. That doesn't take account of the plant-life – you might have Solomon's seal growing in the shade, *Prunella vulgaris* (self-heal) in the lawn, 'Tuscany Superb' in the rose-garden, water hyacinth in the pool and edelweiss in the miniature Alps. These are examples of only one kind of animal or plant in each of only six habitats. You need to multiply them hundreds of times to get an approximation of the diversity that exists both above and in the soil.

USE OF SPRAYS AND FERTILIZERS

Imagine, then, what happens when you destroy the whole population of one of those species of animals or plants – by animals I mean all creatures with life in them that are not plants – and do it in the space of half an hour or so. The balance goes at once, but the knock-on effect goes on and on for weeks, if not months, and the results are devastating. Supposing you then apply several other sprays in quick succession and, not only that, you keep applying them week after week, as you are advised to do to eradicate apple scab or rose black spot, both fungal diseases. The results become catastrophic, because nothing has a chance to recover. As soon as the effects of a spray begin to be diminished, another is used, and another, and another, with cumulative effect, like compound interest extending further and further outside the garden and higher and higher into the atmosphere.

The use of concentrated compounds like fertilizers to increase the quantity of mineral foods in the soil has an even more complicated effect. The chemistry of any type of soil, whether it is essentially a clay, sand, peat, silt, chalk or loam, is exceedingly complex. There are many more ingredients besides these: bacteria and fungi of many different varieties, soil-living insects, worms and spiders, living plant roots, decaying remains of animals and plants, wood, and so on. In addition, there is the variety of particles which make up each grain of soil, to say nothing of the contents of the soil moisture.

If you add relatively large quantities of, for instance, a compound fertilizer containing the three most important plant foods, nitrogen, phosphorus and potassium, the combinations and permutations that can go on as a result can hardly be imagined. Once again, the consequence for the plants and the garden's natural balance is one of major disruption.

Hedgehogs are excellent mobile slug controls.

BENEFITS OF ORGANIC GARDENING

If you garden without using substances which upset this equilibrium, the benefits are enormous. For a start, you can rely on free help in controlling pest numbers which are increasing to the extent that they seriously damage plants: this help will come from various animal sources which include birds, hedgehogs, aquatic creatures, and insects.

BIRDS
There are many birds which are garden-helpers; starlings will search out leather-jackets, the caterpillars of the crane-fly (daddy-long-legs) which feed on the roots of lawn and other grasses. Thrushes are notorious for the vigour with which they bang snails on a hard surface, and tits will winkle out the overwintering eggs of all sorts of so-called insect pests.

HEDGEHOGS
If there is permanent shelter in your garden such as a heap of the most difficult-to-rot-down vegetable rubbish, you might well discover a family of hedgehogs using it as a home, and they are the best walking controls of slugs you will find. A heap of hardwood prunings, small saplings and tough flowering stems piled up late in the summer will provide an ideal hibernating site, and in the spring the inmate(s) will emerge at about the same time as the slugs.

POOLS

A garden with a pool in it will attract frogs and/or toads, because it provides them with somewhere to deposit egg-spawn. The resulting young will remain in the garden, living off a variety of insects, and doing their bit to keep those populations from exploding.

Incidentally, the naturally-occurring ponds in the countryside have mostly disappeared, due to drainage schemes, and this has seriously reduced the toad and frog population because still water is needed for egg production. There are farm reservoirs, but many more areas of water are required, and the larger the better. Pools are high on the list of conservation techniques for gardeners to help save not only frogs and toads, but newts, sticklebacks and many other water creatures.

INSECTS

Insects play one of the largest, if not the largest, parts in controlling the quantities of other insects that the gardener regards as pests. During a hot, dry summer, such as we experienced in 1989, in an unsprayed garden the greenfly (aphids) can be virtually non-existent, while gardens all round it which have been regularly sprayed for years, are awash with them, all over the roses, blackcurrants, lettuce and parsley. The secret lies in allowing their natural predators to live and build up their numbers. This doesn't happen when sprays are used: most aphicides cannot distinguish between predators and their prey.

Ladybirds predate greenfly, and so do their larvae – small creatures which look like tiny black crocodiles (Fig. 1). Hoverfly larvae are voracious predators of aphids of many kinds; and there are at least nine different genera of hoverflies which are a gardener's 'friends'. Many

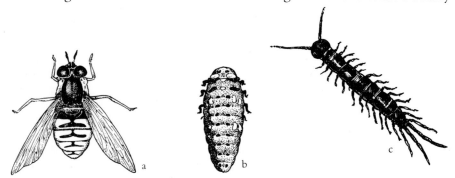

Fig. 1 (*a*) The larvae of hoverflies like this one are predators of greenfly. (*b*) Ladybirds and their small, black, crocodile-like larvae feed on many garden pests such as thrips, scale insects and greenfly. (*c*) Centipedes live in the soil and feed beneath it, on slugs; they are harmless to plants.

adults look like wasps but have blunter, fatter bodies and hover above plants, then dart away to hover somewhere else before diving down to the flowers below. A garden which grows plants attractive to these insects is unlikely to have much trouble with aphids, especially as they tend to lay their eggs on leaves close to aphid colonies.

Caterpillars of all kinds can be another problem, but birds will take a good many of these. Some will not get beyond the egg stage, because they will be eaten before hatching, notably cabbage white butterfly eggs. In many gardens, too, the infestation will be small enough to be collected by hand and fed to the fish, or to ducks or a tame robin.

It's worth remembering, too, that caterpillars can be the forerunners of some beautiful butterflies and moths, and many only feed on wild plants or do so little damage that there is no real harm to the plant. In an unsprayed garden their diversity will increase considerably, particularly if you deliberately plant attractive species of flowers, shrubs and bulbs.

The bee population will increase dramatically as it forages for honey. The honey bee is not a pest, and its presence is highly desirable as it collects honey and distributes pollen from flower to flower, thus ensuring that the fruit grower has heavy crops. Undoubtedly, there will be leaf-cutting bees in an unsprayed garden, removing semi-circular pieces from rose leaves, and also mining bees in the lawn, which industriously excavate holes about 6 in (15 cm) deep, at the bottom of which they lay eggs and leave food for the young when they hatch. But there are so few of both types, they do not do any real harm.

BENEFITS TO SOIL AND PLANT FOOD

Another outstanding advantage in a garden which is managed organically is the maintenance and improvement of the soil structure. Nutrients for plants will be supplied with the application of bulky decayed or decaying organic matter, such as the material from compost heaps or leafmould. This contains humus which ensures that water and air can be present in the soil in the quantities needed by plant roots for good health.

Of course, plants do not obtain all their nutrients from the soil; some are made by the green parts of the plants above ground from the air in the presence of light, during a process called photosynthesis. The end products are oxygen, given off into the atmosphere, and carbohydrates or starches, which are stored or converted within the plant as necessary. The source of these is a combination of carbon dioxide absorbed from the air, and water from within the plant. Most plants consist of at least 80% water.

This helps to explain the concern over the destruction of the rainforests in South America; not only is the oxygen decreased which animals and plants need, to some degree, but carbon dioxide is not used as it would otherwise be. Its percentage share of the atmosphere is now increasing rapidly and is partially responsible for the so-called 'greenhouse effect'.

With improvement in soil formation comes an increase in the numbers and diversity of its living population including the earthworm, which is important for its ability to give soil a good crumb structure, and to introduce drainage channels as it burrows about. No worms in the soil is a very bad sign; other life is highly unlikely to be present in such a soil, and it can be described as 'dead', and of no use at all to plants.

BENEFITS TO THE ENVIRONMENT

The third major benefit is the avoidance of environmental pollution. By refraining from using destructive chemicals, many of which by their very nature need to be long-lasting and in working order for several weeks, or years in the case of weedkillers, the whole internal system of the garden remains 'clean'. Its energy and vigour can flow unimpeded so that all the occupants interact with one another to produce an overall environment high in health and continuity of species.

If you spray insecticides on to plants in order to kill, for instance, red spider mites or whitefly, or drench the roses in a solution intended to ward off black spot; or if you paint jelly on to bindweed ro eradicate it or water the soil with a cabbage root-fly eliminator; all the substances in these powders and solutions will find their way to some degree into the soil water, which drains out of the garden into streams and rivers, and eventually into the sea. On the way, a part of every substance will be deposited, so that both the soil and water ouside your property boundaries will be polluted, and the natural equilibrium upset on a much larger scale, and with much greater consequences.

It is worth remembering, too, that although there are chemical controls currently advised as being harmless, this description only holds good in the light of present knowledge. DDT was thought to be the answer to any problem relating to overpopulation of insects, until, that is, its persistence and effect on birds were discovered; more recently the selective (hormone) weedkiller 2,4,5-T has been banned because of the discovery that it can contain dioxin, the material used to spray the Vietnamese forests. In spite of trials, testing, and experiment, many chemicals are recommended as being safe after only a few years' research — a lifetime is really needed to discover whether they are truly safe. Even that is only a compromise, when you consider the hundreds of thousands of

Birds will be attracted into a garden by berry-bearing plants such as this variegated holly, *Ilex* × *altaclarensis* 'Golden King'.

years it has taken for the variety of life that can now be found in gardens to evolve and maintain the precious natural balance with which we are concerned.

Instead of following the current standard practices for eradicating and killing unwanted occupants of the garden, you can substitute a plan which takes account of your natural allies, and includes organic substances and cultural techniques which side-step potential damage to plants. You cannot eliminate all pollution because some comes from outside sources, such as industrial emissions and motor transport exhaust, but pollution in the garden will be considerably diminished by your efforts, and the environment outside it will be cleaner, too, and by an impressive degree, if more gardeners pursued organic principles.

Table 1.1 Berry-bearing plants which will attract birds to the garden

Aucuba japonica – Japanese laurel
Berberis darwinii – barberry
Cotoneaster horizontalis – fishbone cotoneaster
Crataegus species – hawthorn
Euonymus europaeus – spindle tree
Hippophae rhamnoides (female form) – sea buckthorn
Ilex aquifolium – holly
Lonicera periclymenum (early and late flowering varieties) – honeysuckle
Pernettya mucronata – pernettya
Pyracantha coccinea 'Lalandei' – firethorn
Sambucus nigra – elderberry
Sorbus aucuparia – mountain ash, rowan
Symphoricarpos varieties – snowberry
Taxus baccata – yew
Viburnum lantana – wayfaring tree
V. opulus – guelder rose

Table 1.2 Birds

The following birds eat a variety of food which includes insects of all kinds, berries and fruits, worms, spiders, slugs and snails, buds, and seeds, including weed seeds. Leaving the seedheads on ornamentals may look untidy but it attracts a greater variety of birds, for instance the goldfinch lives chiefly on thistle seeds.

Blackbird	Goldfinch	Magpie	Starling	Thrush	Wagtail
Blackcap	House martin	Robin	Swallow	Tit	Woodpecker
Fieldfare	Jackdaw	Sparrow	Swift	Tree creeper	Wren

Table 1.3 Plants to attract bees

Alyssum	*Limnanthes douglasii* – bee flower
Berberis – barberry	Lupinus – lupin
Borago officinalis – borage	*Melissa officinalis* – lemon balm
Cheiranthus – wallflower	Narcissus
Cotoneaster horizontalis – fishbone cotoneaster	*Origanum vulgare* – marjoram
	Nepeta – catmint
Clarkia	*Pulmonaria officinalis* – lungwort
Crocus	*Salvia officinalis* – sage
Delphinium	Satureia – savory
Digitalis purpurea – foxglove	Scabiosa – scabious
Eryngium maritimum – sea holly	Sedum – ice plant
Godetia	Tamarix – tamarisk
Hyssopus officinalis – hyssop	*Thymus vulgaris, T. serpyllum*
Iberis – candytuft	– common and creeping thyme
Lavandula – lavender	

Table 1.4 Cultivated plants to attract butterflies searching for nectar

Armeria maritima – thrift	Lavandula – lavender
Aster novae-angliae – Michaelmas daisy	*Limonium vulgare* – sea lavender
A. novi-belgii – Michaelmas daisy	*Lonicera periclymenum* – honeysuckle
Alyssum	*Lunaria annua* – honesty
Arabis	*Origanum vulgare* – wild marjoram
Aubrieta	*Nepeta × faassenii* – catmint
Buddleia in variety	Phlox
Caryopteris × clandonensis	*Reseda odorata* – mignonette
Coreopsis	*Rosmarinus officinalis* – rosemary
Cosmea	Rubus – blackberry
Dianthus barbatus – sweet william	Scabiosa – scabious
Heliotropium – heliotrope	*Sedum spectabile* – ice plant
Hyssopus officinalis – hyssop	Syringa – lilac
Iberis – candytuft	Thymus – thyme

CHAPTER 2

STARTING THE RIGHT WAY WITH PLANTS

You can give your plants a good deal of help for the rest of their life if you start them off correctly. On the other hand, a bad beginning can result in an unhealthy adult plant, and it may even be that the plant dies before it matures. Taking a lot of care in the early stages pays tremendous dividends, not only in the plant's general health, but in the improvement of its appearance, its size, and its production of crops. You will also save trouble later on because less time will be taken up with constant spraying, feeding and general nursing.

There are several different aspects to getting a plant off to a good start, each of which will be covered in this and the next three chapters, but there is one which is fundamental to all plants, regardless of the way in which they are cultivated.

PLANTS AND PLACES

Garden centres are notoriously difficult places in which to resist impulse buying, and almost everyone can probably think of a time they went into one and brought away a plant which they had no intention of buying originally. Then comes the problem of fitting it into the garden. You may have thought at the time of buying that 'it would look good in such and such a place', or that 'it will just fill that difficult corner nicely', but nine times out of ten the unfortunate plant will end up in surroundings which are totally alien to it.

Plants are like people in that different groups feel more comfortable in certain environments; some people cannot stand the heat and go on holiday to Scandinavia, others revel in it and are only really happy in temperatures of 32°C (90°F) or more. Any living thing will have characteristics which make it different from other individuals; and with evolution has come the development of groups of individuals which have some broadly similar requirements. Plants certainly have a good deal of life in them and have adapted to their surroundings, whatever they are, in order to survive. Some surroundings have such marked qualities about them that they can be termed 'habitats'.

Plants will only grow with difficulty, or even not at all, in sites which

One of the best bee plants is *Digitalis purpurea*, the foxglove, a most decorative garden plant as well.

are very unlike their native habitat. One extreme example of a habitat is a salt marsh, where the land is regularly flooded with tidal salt water every day. The flora in it is unique to its environment, such as *Glaux maritima* (sea milkwort), which you may sometimes find as a 'weed' in sea-washed turf, or *Limonium vulgare* (sea lavender), which has been crossed by the plant-breeders to produce varieties with pretty garden flowers capable of growing in garden soil.

If you do buy a plant on impulse, without knowing anything about it, you should be able to obtain help with its cultivation from the information on the label, some of which will recommend the place in which to grow it. If this is not available, ask an assistant, and if he or she cannot help, do not go to that garden centre again! In such a case a general gardening encyclopaedia will be the best source of advice; a useful one is recommended at the end of this book, which can either be bought, or borrowed from a public library. Such a book will give the plant's country of origin, and from this you can get clues as to the temperature and aspect to which the plant was accustomed. Every garden will have its own mini-habitats, and once you have sorted these out, you can choose plants that are not only suited to them, but which fit your colour, design and seasonal requirements as well. But if you must impulse-buy, and a lot of fun in gardening comes from seeing a plant which instantly appeals and buying it, at least find out what it needs environmentally before you plant.

NEEDS OF PLANTS

Environmental qualities which are of particular importance to plants are:
- the amount of light they receive and hence the degree of shadiness of the site
- the type of soil
- the average temperature of the garden, and that of the site
- the amount of shelter or exposure to wind
- the kinds of plants being grown near them

LIGHT

Quantity and quality can make or break a plant; some need as much intense sun as possible all day, e.g. helianthemum (sun-roses); at the other extreme are those requiring shade, for example *Helleborus niger* (Christmas rose). Some like dappled shade, that is, sun filtering through the branches of trees, such as lilies and foxgloves; some simply like an open aspect facing north, which is not a sun-trap, but which is not shadowed; the clematis 'Nelly Moser' has much deeper coloured flowers in such a position.

SOIL

The soil in which they grow should also suit them, and the biggest divide between plants in this respect is between those liking acid soil, such as rhododendrons, and those liking alkaline (often chalky) soil, such as scabious. Some need plenty of moisture all the time, as do primulas, others, such as lavender, die unless the soil is often dry.

TEMPERATURE

Temperature, the degree of warmth or cold, can mean life or death to a plant. Many are hardy – that is, they will continue to live in spite of frost and snow – but equally as many plants grown in temperate climates come from sub-tropical zones, and need a protective covering in winter; even so, some of them can be frozen to death. In this respect every garden will have areas in it which are always warmer than others, or sites in which the snow and frost linger longest, called frost-pockets.

WIND

Wind can have as devastating an effect as drought, high temperatures or frost on a plant. Constant exposure to it for some of them will brown and dry up the edges of leaves, flowers, buds and soft green stems, warp their growth permanently, stunt them, and if it is a winter wind with a strong chill factor in it, will kill them if it continues for long enough. Some can stand up to wind, coastal plants in particular; some cannot, and these are often plants growing naturally far inland or protected in forests.

NEARBY PLANTS

Unsuitable neighbouring plants will be large vigorous ones growing close to small varieties, or climbing plants with no support other than their neighbours, though sometimes this doesn't matter, if the neighbour is stout and well-anchored, for instance clematis growing up through a small tree. Some plants are thought to ensure good growth in other plants if grown close to them – this is called companion planting – and an example is planting sage and rosemary side by side.

NEW PLANTS AND HEALTH

There are all sorts of ways in which you can stock your garden; new plants can come from seed, rooted cuttings, budding or grafting, dividing existing plants, layering and so on. With all these you will know the source, but they will only reproduce to a large extent the varieties you have already in the garden. To obtain new ones, you will need to go to garden centres, nurseries, chain stores and garden shops. You can also obtain them from charity events, or as gifts from friends.

If you can, when you are looking at plants from any of these outlets, pick a strong healthy one with good colouring. Make sure all its stems are intact, the leaves undamaged and bright green, or well variegated, and choose one which is in bud, not in flower; look for the specimen with the largest number of buds. It will establish better, and the subsequent flower display will last longer. Try to buy a plant whose roots are not coiled round the base of the container or protruding through the drainage holes. Above all, buy one which is free of pests and disease – it will be a really bad start if greenfly or white powdery mildew are already infecting the stems and leaves. If a friend gives you a plant, obviously you cannot reject it out of hand if it is weak or infested, but isolate it for a time and give it extra care. You may be able to take a cutting or layer it in due course.

If there are any sources of plants in your area which grow organically, use these rather than the inorganic plant suppliers. There are more likely to be organic vegetable and fruit stockists than ornamental plant nurserymen; organically grown seeds can also be obtained (see Appendix for names and addresses).

CHAPTER 3

STARTING THE RIGHT WAY WITH SOIL

The soil is a plant's life-support system, a fact which seems obvious enough since it acts as an anchor for the roots. But it is also a source of much of its food, and of practically all its water. If either of these is in short supply, for whatever reason, the plant will not thrive, and will often actually die. The state of your garden is dependent on the state of the soil in it, and the type of plant you can grow will depend on the type of soil. The depth of soil is also important. As an organic gardener you have much more control over the garden's soil, and you can do a great deal more to get it into good condition than an inorganic gardener.

WHAT IS SOIL?

Soil is a living organism, just as much as a plant is, and should be treated accordingly. It is not just dirt, something which makes a mess of one's hands, but a substance consisting of a vast mass of ingredients; myriads of bacteria of different kinds, species of fungi, soil-living insects such as caterpillars, beetles, centipedes, spiders and slugs, worms of all sorts, to say nothing of moles and voles.

The soil itself consists of all sorts of particles having different chemical make-ups, depending on whether they are sand, clay, silt, chalk and so on. They differ in size, and the way in which they hold together to make larger particles, which in turn are bound together into the crumbs which are typical of a good soil structure. Water is another major constituent, which keeps all these and everything else in working order, and without which everything comes to a grinding halt. You could almost regard it as the equivalent of oil in an engine. There is also a constantly changing mass of vegetation of various kinds, some of it decaying, some of it living, which is being worked on by the soil insects, bacteria, etc., to produce an end product called humus. This does so much to keep the soil in good heart that no healthy soil can survive without it.

HUMUS
Humus is a somewhat mysterious substance which quite simply consists of small, dark brown to black particles, the residue resulting from the soil

creatures feeding on the decaying vegetable and animal remains in the soil. When dry, it is powdery; when wet the particles swell up and become jelly-like because it is, technically speaking, a colloid. It is this property which does so much to alter the structure of a soil.

Humus is always obtained from decaying organic matter, and this is why it is so important to make sure your soil contains such material. In the natural way of things, it would accumulate of it own accord by such processes as the autumn leaf-fall, the breaking of branches and shoots in gales, the decay of flowers and stems as a plant reaches the end of its life, and the death of insects, worms and other animal soil inhabitants. But the average garden is constantly being tidied, so that all the dead seed-heads, scattered leaves, and dead mice left by the cat are never left to rot away *in situ* but are thrown on to the bonfire and burnt. Consequently the soil becomes starved of its life-force, and this state is reflected in the plants.

ORGANIC MATTER

No garden will be healthy, beautiful and productive unless its soil is regularly fed several times a year with rotting organic matter to supply the precious humus described earlier. The most important kinds of organic matter include: farm manure from pigsties, cowsheds and stables; garden compost made in compost heaps; spent mushroom compost left from commercial mushroom cultivation; leafmould; seaweed; and peat. Others which can be used are: composted bark, straw, sawdust, spent hops and wood shavings, mostly cheaper but less useful.

The most important one for you as an organic gardener will be the

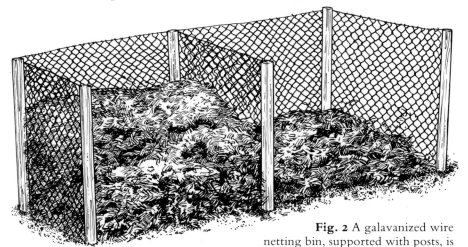

Fig. 2 A galavanized wire netting bin, supported with posts, is suitable for collecting leaves to rot down into leafmould.

Sow this annual *Limnanthes douglasii* for aphid control, as it attracts the predatory hoverflies in large numbers.

garden compost, closely followed by leafmould (Fig.2), because these are both free, and because the recycling that results enables the garden to be self-sufficient. All the sources of organic matter in the first list will contain plant mineral foods varying in quantity and quality, but always in useful amounts; those in the second list will contain little and, more-over, take a long time – one or more years – to rot adequately.

COMPOST HEAPS

Any garden which is suitably cared for will be controlled so that the plants don't take over and surround the house with jungle. The resulting surplus plant material forms the major ingredient of a compost heap (to compost is to combine by putting two or more things together) which helps in two ways: you obtain your organic matter without paying for it, and keep the garden clear of what used to be called rubbish.

You can put all kinds of soft vegetable material on the heap: the remains of vegetable crops, leaves, green hedge clippings, flowers, weeds, provided they are not the real nasties (see pp.91–92), grass mowings and soft prunings. The remains of fruit and vegetables left from preparing food in the kitchen make a surprisingly appreciable addition to the heap; tea leaves and coffee grounds are of course vegetable remains as well.

The quicker you can build the heap the better, as it is more likely to generate the heat required to kill fungi, the potential causes of disease, and seeds (including weed seeds). Its size should be at least 90 × 90 × 90 cm (3 × 3 × 3 ft); in a smaller heap there is usually not enough material to produce the high temperatures of 60°C (140°F) and more that are required. You can contain it in a slatted wooden bin, plastic bins with

Fig. 3 (*a*) A double compost bin made with wooden slats, which are removable at the front, allows one binful to rot down while the other is being filled. (*b*) Lines of bricks provide air channels at the base of the heap, and help to ventilate the interior. (*c*) If the weather and material for the heap are dry, water each layer thoroughly as the heap is built. (*d*) (*i*) A plastic compost bin in which the panels slide up and down and the cover is hinged to fold in half. (*ii*) Another type of plastic bin with a neatly fitting lid, in brown or green; it must have aeration at the base.

lids, wire bins lined with cardboard or in bales of straw, or you can build it directly on the ground and cover it with a heavy duty black plastic sheet (Fig. 3).

Always remember that there are two essentials for successful rotting of compost heaps: air and moisture. When you build a bonfire, you make sure there is air going in under the material and then up through it, to keep the fire burning, and the same principle applies to compost heaps (Fig. 4). So raise the heap slightly off the ground with rows of bricks, or a few woody shoots and small branches or cabbage and brussels sprouts stalks, and build it round a vertical pole or poles, then remove them when the heap is finished.

You should also make sure that it remains moist. In a dry heap much of the material becomes mummified and provides a home for hedgehogs, woodlice or wasps. This is why heaps contained with unlined wire netting are so bad; the sides rapidly become dry and never rot, and the

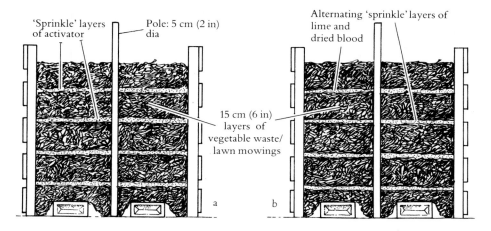

Fig. 4 Building a compost heap: the central pole is put in at the beginning and the material piled round it, then removed when the heap is completed. (*a*) Using an activator. (*b*) Using alternate 'layers' of lime and dried blood.

centre is prone to do the same. Cover the top with a plastic sheet, several thicknesses of sacking, or use an old piece of carpet.

Air and moisture will ensure that bacteria can live and feed, and break down the organic material, but they will also need nutrients, particularly nitrogen. Often there will be sufficient already present in the heap, but you can add what is called an activator containing the necessary minerals, for instance Q.R. or Fertosan. In two to six months the heap should consist of dark brown, moist, crumbly material, none of which looks at all like the original ingredients.

TYPES OF SOIL

It is important to know what kind of soil you have in the garden, as plants have their preferences, and what is good for one is bad for another. The two main types are clay soil and sandy soil: that is, soils which have either more clay particles in them than anything else, or more sand. Both can be considerably modified so that the clay or sand content is hardly noticeable.

To distinguish between the two, notice how quickly rain or irrigation water drains through them. A hole dug in a clay soil about 30 cm (1 ft) deep and filled with water will still have some left half an hour later, but a sandy hole will be empty. Another test is the feel of the soil: clay will be distinctly sticky when wet, sandy ones will feel gritty when rubbed between the fingers. A third indication of the soil type is the presence of cracks in a clay one during dry weather, and its tendency to stick to the spade when being dug.

Other soil types include the peaty kind, dark coloured and rather spongy; chalky, silty, which feels rather smooth and slimy when wet, and very slightly sticky, and the best kind of all, a good loam, which has a balance of all the types of particles described, together with rotting organic matter and humus. Such a soil is usually crumbly, nearly always moist, easy to work, and dark in colour.

The plant foods present in these soils will vary in amounts and numbers, depending on the soil. A clay soil which has been cultivated and well looked after will be rich in nutrients, but a sandy one in which the water washes through it, rapidly and easily, will have the nutrients washed through, too. Chalk tends to be starved of everything but calcium; peat is often short of all the plant foods except for a little nitrogen; silt is sometimes very rich.

One more point you should know about your soil, and that is whether it is acid or alkaline. Chalky soils will obviously be alkaline, but so are some clay types, and also silt; sandy ones, loam, and peaty kinds are often acid – in fact anything which has a lot of organic matter in it, such as peat, is generally acid. You can test to see whether it is one or the other with a simple soil-testing kit (Fig. 5). Look in your local garden centre or garden shop for one. The kit will tell you how much lime to add if the soil is very acid.

A slightly acid value suits the majority of plants very well; very alkaline soils need to be planted with carefully chosen varieties, since modifying them can take years, and requires a great deal of rotting vegetable material. Only acid soils are suitable for rhododendrons, azaleas, most heathers, and a variety of other shrubs in the heather family (*Ericaceae*), together with some flowering border perennials and bulbs.

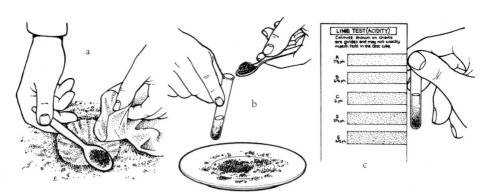

Fig. 5 (*a*) Testing the soil for its degree of acidity; collect samples without touching them with the hands. (*b*) Add soil carefully to the tube containing the indicator solution. (*c*) Compare the colour of the shaken solution after it has settled with the chart supplied with the kit.

To encourage butterflies to come into the garden, plant a buddleia, a quick-growing, late summer-flowering shrub.

PLANT FOODS AND FERTILIZERS

Practically everything that exists needs food to help it survive. Everything, even minerals and metals, gives off energy, and some sort of substance is needed to fuel it. For plants this food consists of particles of minerals (as well as that made during photosynthesis, see p. 13) which are present in the soil. In order that the plant can 'eat' them, they must be contained in the soil moisture, because its roots absorb this moisture as one of the necessities of existence.

Mineral nutrients are found in particles of different rocks, ground down by weathering in the course of millions of years to microscopic fragments. Each nutrient is an element, that is it cannot be separated any further to produce another substance. Amongst the most important elements for plants are nitrogen phosphorus and potassium, sometimes called 'the big three'. Many fertilizers, inorganic or organic, consist of these three in varying proportions.

Each is the fuel for different parts and activities of the plant, just as protein in animals is necessary for making new tissue, and calcium ensures good bones and teeth. Nitrogen (abbreviated to N) is essential for stem and leaf growth, phosphorus (P) is concerned with root development and maturity of seeds and fruits, and potassium (K) regulates the water conditions and various other processes within the plant. This is a very simple and generalized explanation of what these minerals are used for; they all have many other functions, and interact with one another.

Besides these three, there are other minerals essential to plant growth, but not required in such large amounts. Indeed, the quantities are so small that they are called trace elements, and include manganese, boron, molybdenum. There are at least ten of them. Two more elements, iron and calcium, are called intermediate or minor, being between the two kinds as regards quantity and importance. Altogether 15 elements are known to be essential to plant growth at present; there are others found in plants, such as silicon and vanadium, which may also prove to be essential, and like the big three, all have a particular function or functions.

On the whole, there is no need to add the trace and minor elements to garden soils; they are required in such small amounts that what is already there is sufficient. The big three are more important, and may need to be provided.

ORGANIC FERTILIZERS

Although bulky organic manures contain plant food, it is in varying amounts, and on the whole there is not a great deal of it in them. The intensive cropping that occurs with vegetable and fruit growing usually needs a boost from special plant food dressings; roses often need extra food; quick-draining, sandy or chalky soils are perennially starved; lawns take a heavy beating with top growth removal; and there is nearly always an odd corner or three where nothing will grow, unless fertilizers are supplied. Town garden soils need feeding initially and often continue to need treatment thereafter.

Table 3.1 Organic fertilizers

Fertilizer	Nutrient	Rate of application g/sq m (oz/sq yd)
Blood, fish and bone	nitrogen, phosphorus, potassium	90–120 (3–4)
Bonemeal	phosphorus, a little potassium	90 (3)
Dried blood (quick acting)	nitrogen	60 (2)
Dried seaweed	major and trace elements	60 (2)
Hoof and horn	nitrogen	60–120 (2–4)
Wood ash (quick acting)	potassium, alkaline	120–240 (4–8)

There is also now available an organic form of the inorganic compound fertilizer Growmore; this contains nitrogen, phosphorus and potassium to a given analysis of: N 6%, P 8%, K 4%.

A substance not so far mentioned which can also be considered to be an organic fertilizer, is lime, since it is derived from natural chalk and is not manufactured, and since the calcium it contains is an essential nutrient, part of whose use is to form cell walls. Lime is chalk; hydrated lime (calcium hydroxide) has had water added to it, chalk (calcium carbonate) acts less quickly, ground limestone (limestone flour, also calcium carbonate), is slower still in its action, and quicklime (calcium oxide) is quick-acting but caustic, and should only be used on vacant ground. Gypsum (calcium sulphate) has the same effect as chalk, but is neutral, not alkaline, so is a good form to use on alkaline soils.

TREATING THE SOIL

To improve the structure of the soil and keep it in good condition, bulky organics should be provided annually, first by digging in, and secondly by mulching.

DIGGING

Digging is mainly done in the autumn and early winter, sometimes also in early-mid spring, to prepare the soil for the new season's vegetables, and for permanent plantings of fruit, perennials, trees and shrubs, and bulbs. Rates of application vary a good deal, depending on the plant and soil type, and time of year, but the following can be used as a starting point, and modified in the light of experience. Whatever you use, the method is to spread it on the soil surface and fork or spade it in, mixing it thoroughly as you go. If double-digging, that is, digging two spades deep, mix it into the forked-up soil at the base of the hole or trench, return the lowest one spade's depth of soil, spread organic matter over it and fork it into it, and repeat with the next one. This will be the topsoil with a better structure, and will need a little less.

Seaweed will be very wet, so use a really waterproof container if you are transporting it from the beach by car. The salt in it will be broken down during the autumn and winter but, if used in spring, it is better to spread it out and water it well before digging it in. It can also be added to compost heaps, when it should be mixed really thoroughly with the other materials.

Straw and sawdust are sometimes advised for use by organic gardeners for improving soil, but both need a good deal of rotting down, and it is quite possible to dig them in during their fresh state and find them quite

Table 3.2 Rates of application of organic matter to different soil types

Organic matter	sand, chalk	clay, silt	loam, peat
		kg/sq m (lb/sq yd)	
Garden compost, farm manure	7/15	4.5/10	5.5/12
Peat	5.5/12 initially, then 4/9	2.75/6	4/9
Seaweed (fresh)	9/20	4.5/10	7/15
Leafmould	2.75/6★	2.25/5	2/4
Composted bark	better not dug in as can carry fungus disease		
Spent mushroom compost	3.75/8	2/4	2.75/6

★In 2nd year leafmould is alkaline, but if oak and ash leaves are used these will reduce alkalinity.

untouched at the end of the winter. Moreover, straw has often been con-taminated by chemical weedkillers and pesticides applied by the farmer, and some residue will be present. They are better used as mulches, and preferably only if you can find a local organic farmer. Composted bark also makes a good mulch and, when finely divided, is an excellent ingredient of potting composts, to replace some of the peat.

MULCHING

Mulching is an easier method of using bulky organics as it consists simply of spreading them over the soil surface round plants and along rows, and leaving it there to rot down and be naturally assimilated. The benefits of this are many:

- keeps the soil moist
- supplies plant food
- maintains and improves the soil structure
- encourages earthworms
- prevents weed growth
- prevents soil erosion and exposure of roots
- protects tender plants against cold
- prevents compaction of the soil surface

All the materials listed for digging in can be used except fresh seaweed – this is smelly as it dries, and when dry is thin and papery. Straw, saw-dust, spent hops and wood shavings can also be used, the first-named

Plants grown in the right place will thrive, as these flowering plants are, in their sunny border.

being especially good round soft fruit, but it is advisable to mix a sprinkling of a nitrogenous fertilizer with them, such as dried blood or hoof and horn, otherwise bacteria will use soil nitrogen in breaking them down, and rob the mulched plants.

Thickness of a mulch is about 5–7.5 cm (2–3 in), though fruit and roses may need a 15-cm (6-in) depth. As a general principle the poorer the soil the more mulch is required. Time to apply is preferably mid to end of late spring, putting the mulch on to moist soil, not dry, which is weed-free, spread evenly all over the area concerned, remembering that roots spread at least as far underground as the canopy of shoots and branches above ground. Protective mulches are put on to crowns of tender plants before the first frosts, and they too need to be 15 cm (6 in) and more deep.

FEEDING
Fertilizers can be applied from late winter to late spring; the slow-acting

kinds first, the fast ones such as dried blood and dried seaweed, later in spring and even into summer, but not after the beginning of late summer. Sprinkle them on to the soil surface evenly along rows and round plants, so that all of a given area gets its share, then fork them in, and water if rain is not forecast.

Lime can be used to ameliorate markedly acid soil, and the rate of application for different soil types will be indicated with the soil-testing kit. Rates vary between 120g (4 oz) and 1 kg (2.2 lb) per sq m (sq yd), depending on the type of soil, degree of acidity, and degree of change required. Apply it some weeks before or after dressing with bulky organics, never at the same time, otherwise the nitrogen in the organic material reacts with the lime and is given off as ammonia. Sprinkle the lime evenly over the soil, and leave it to be weathered in.

Town garden soils   There are still a good many gardens in towns and cities. They can easily have been there for several hundred years, but unfortunately have not been looked after. With the accumulation of soot and other air pollutants, bird droppings, cat and dog excretion and general rubbish, the original soil has become dirt: sooty, powdery and completely dead. These town soils need extra special treatment to get them back into working order. To get any results in the first season you will have to add inorganic fertilizers.

At the same time dig in as much organic matter of any kind, from whatever source. Parks departments can supply leaves in autumn; zoos often have litter to dispose of, local councils may have treated sewage schemes in operation, your country friends can be a source of supply of straw and manure, and peat is always available from garden stores and centres. Some of the new growth that results from the use of the inorganic ferilizers in the first season can be used for compost heaps, as well as the material from the general clearing up and pruning that is likely to be necessary.

In the second season use inorganic fertilizers to start with in the early spring, and in mid to late spring mix in the organic kinds. By this time, with the addition of organic matter, including that from last season's compost heap, life should be coming back into the soil, and the nutrients in slow-acting organic fertilizers like blood-fish-and-bone, or hoof and horn, will be broken down by bacteria and made available for your plants. Even so, vegetables, lawns and roses may still need boosting with inorganics. By the third season, the soil should be well on the way back to being fertile, friable and a good home for your plants, and should no longer require anything but organic materials. But be prepared for recovery to take up to five years.

CHAPTER 4

PLANTS AND PLANTING

If you are intending to grow all your plants organically, you will be doing them and yourself a great service in the future by taking care over their planting. It is easy to see a plant at a garden centre, buy it, go home and dig a hole, push the plant in and fill round it with soil, then stamp it in and water it. But the chances of that plant surviving are fairly remote, especially if you do this in summer. If it does manage to survive, the great effort it will have had to make will have weakened it, and as a mature plant it will then be much more badly infested by pests, and the roots in particular can easily succumb to heavy rain and/or cold. When you consider the cost of even a small plant as well, it doesn't make sense to go to all that trouble and expense – extra for sprays later on – when this could be avoided with a little advance thinking.

SOIL PREPARATION

It is a rare garden soil that is fit to receive a plant without any advance warning; at the very least the planting site will need to be weeded. If the weeds are perennials like bindweed or ground elder, digging will be essential, and every single scrap of weed root must be removed, otherwise they will sprout and grow inextricably amongst the new plant, so that you will either have to dig it up or use weedkiller.

While digging, you can mix in rotted organic matter and remove stones and rubbish at the same time. Depth and size of hole will depend on the type of plant (see pp. 35, 37). This initial preparation should be done several weeks in advance of planting, to allow the soil time to settle and begin to absorb the added material. Then, seven to ten days before planting, fork in a fertilizer, either a compound such as organic Grow-more, or blood, fish and bone. Never add a fertilizer at the same time as planting – neat fertilizer is liable to scorch the roots and do more harm than good. Add it in advance and water the soil immediately afterwards.

PLANTING

The best times to plant are mid-autumn and late autumn while the soil is still warm, followed by mid-spring when growth is starting, though the soil will be cold. The winter is unlikely to be suitable, but plants will survive summer planting if really well watered, except conifers, whose planting then is very risky.

In general when planting, make sure the plant is really firm in the ground. Until it develops its anchor roots, different from the feeding roots, its main support will be the firmness of the soil around the roots or root-ball. If need be, use your foot to compress the soil. Depth of planting should be such that the soil-mark on the stem or stems, or the surface of the root-ball, is level with the surface of the surrounding soil.

Once planted, rake the soil round the plant, and then mulch with rotted organic matter in a circle around it. Keep the mulch clear of the stem, otherwise it can encourage decay of the bark,and mice may nest there and eat the bark. Water in well, unless the soil is already fairly moist, and if the soil is dry, give the planting site a soaking before planting.

CONTAINER PLANTS

Most plants are sold as container plants from garden centres, which means that they can be planted at any time of the year, provided the soil is not frozen, waterlogged or covered with snow. The compost in the container and the roots form a root-ball (soil-ball) which can be planted complete, so the roots never suffer the shock of being forcibly torn out of the soil. They should therefore be able to establish much more quickly than those dug out of the soil at a nursery, and this is why they can be planted pretty well all year round.

However, there are one or two points to note when planting them. First, remove the container! If sheet plastic, slit it down one side, if rigid plastic, push it off, or bang the edge gently on a firm surface. If there are long roots coiled round at the base of the root-ball, cut them back level with it. Loosen the sides and base of the ball a little, make sure the compost is moist and remove any weeds from the surface. If the root-ball is dry, leave it in a bucket of water until thoroughly soaked through to the centre. Fill with soil around it in the hole and compress it so that it is compacted to the same degree as the compost of the root-ball, otherwise the roots will not develop new growth and push out into the surrounding soil.

OPEN-GROUND PLANTS

Before garden centres appeared on the scene, plants were always grown in the ground at nurseries and then dug up as ordered, with a few exceptions for plants that took unkindly to root disturbance. There are a good many nurseries which still do this, sending out the plants 'bare-rooted', and this does have advantages. The roots never become cramped and strangled, nor are they permanently bent into unnatural positions. One of the biggest drawbacks to growing healthy adult plants is that container-grown specimens often finish up with distorted roots through being in the container far too long before being sold.

Another advantage is that all the soil that surrounds them in the planting hole is the same as that in the surrounding ground, and the roots do not have to adapt to a new growing medium, nor is there the risk of the root-ball acting as a kind of sump.

When planting bare-root plants, cut any torn ones back cleanly and then spread them out as naturally as possible in the hole to their full length. Crumble the soil in over them, firm it as you go, and make sure there are no air pockets beneath the centre: it should rest on soil, not a vacuum.

DIFFERENT KINDS OF PLANTS

SHRUBS, TREES, CLIMBERS, ROSES, FRUIT TREES, BUSH AND CANE FRUIT, CONIFERS

Size of hole for all these should be about 60 cm (2 ft) each way, if square, or 60 cm (2 ft) in circumference if round, and 30–45 cm (1–1½) deep. Use a bucketful of organic matter to each site, and fertilizer at the rates recommended on p. 30.

You may find that roses, if grown in containers, are 'duck-footed', that is, the roots have been bundled together and then pushed into the container so that the lower half of the roots is at right angles to the upper half, like an 'L'. This is what happens when the plant is not grown in a container from the start. There is little that can be done to improve their shape, but you can at least try spreading them out, and resolve never to go to that source of supply again. Plant roses so that union between stock and variety, a bump low down on the stem, is a little below soil level, otherwise the rootstock will sprout and take over the top growth.

Conifers, rhododendrons and azaleas, heathers and a few other shrubs may be sent from a nursery with the root-ball wrapped in hessian. Apart from slitting this down one side when the plant is in position, do not remove it as it will rot away naturally.

All trees (Fig. 6), especially standards, should have a supporting stake, rammed into the hole before planting. Attach the trunk to it with planting ties or soft string padded with nylon tights or sacking. If trees suffer from wind-rock after planting, a hollow will form in the soil around the base of the stem, and when this fills with water, rotting of the bark and wood at soil level is likely. Provide wire netting or plastic guards to

Fig. 6 Giving a bare-rooted tree the right start. Put the tree close to the stake so that it can be firmly tied and supported; use a board to ensure the correct planting depth.

prevent rabbits and deer from eating the bark of trees.

Fruit trees should be planted with the point of union of scion (variety) and rootstock several cm (in) above the soil, otherwise the scion may root and bypass the effects of the stock on its vigour and earliness of fruiting.

HERBACEOUS PERENNIALS

When preparing the planting sites, there is no need to dig the large holes recommended for woody plants; 38 × 30 cm (15 × 12 in) will be sufficient for most varieties. Some perennials have markedly fleshy roots, and these need to be handled carefully because, if bruised or injured, they can be infectd by rot entering the damaged part. The crowns of perennials should be level with the soil surface (the crown is the junction between roots and top growth.)

BULBS

The easiest of all to plant. The main point to remember is that the depth of soil covering them should be the same as the length of the bulb. If a bulb is 2.5 cm (1 in) long, it should have 2.5 cm (1 in) depth of soil above it – the planting hole should therefore be 5 cm (2 in) deep (Fig. 7). Bulbs like good drainage, so it does no harm to put a little coarse sand in the base of the hole. Do not mix organic matter with the soil when preparing it. Bulbs do best where such material was applied for a previous planting. Hence soil preparation need only be done about ten days in advance, by forking over the site and mixing in a little balanced, compound, organic fertilizer.

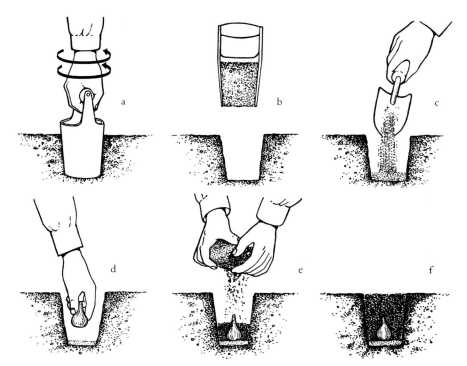

Fig. 7 Planting bulbs
(*a*) Use a planter to take out cores of soil; it will be calibrated on the side to various depths. (*b*) The core of soil is removed complete, to leave a smooth-sided hole. (*c*) Add a little sand to the base of the hole to improve drainage. (*d*) Place the bulb gently in the base without pressing it down. (*e*) Fill in crumbled soil from the removed core, mixed with a little peat if the soil is at all heavy. (*f*) The planted bulb.

SMALL PLANTS, INCLUDING STRAWBERRIES AND ROCK PLANTS

Plant as for perennials, but the planting sites need not be dug out individually and digging need only be to one spade's depth. Small plants are vulnerable to lack of water, so make doubly sure to give them a good watering in, and water the soil well before planting, if it is dry. Rock plants will establish better if a light mulch of gravel can be used around them rather than organic material.

AFTERCARE

The most important point is to make sure the newly set plants are never short of water, particularly if planted from containers in summer. Conifers will need watering every evening, so will vegetable transplants such as those of the cabbage family, and conifers should also be sprayed overhead with clear water daily unless rain occurs. Keep an eye on stakes, to make sure they are doing their job, and replace scattered mulches.

CHAPTER 5

SEEDS AND SOWING

It is just as important to start the right way when growing plants from seed, as it is when you use young plants as a starting point. Plants grown from seed sown by you will be ultimately stronger and healthier than bought-in plants, though the process of raising them from seed takes more time and attention.

Such plants will be used to your garden's climate and soil from the beginning of their lives. They will not have to adjust to a different environment, and you will be able to transplant them from containers, if need be, at exactly the right time, before the roots and soil are damagingly compacted. Furthermore, you can keep an eagle eye on their day-to-day growth and, if any pests or diseases appear on one or two plants, deal with them straightaway before they do any real damage or infect other plants. You can also be sure that they have had an organic start with the soil or compost.

If you want to grow your seeds organically right from the start, you can obtain seeds which have themselves been produced from organically-grown plants. There are one or two suppliers of this type of seed, names and addresses of which are given in the appendix together with those of inorganic seed suppliers.

SOWING SEED OUTDOORS

Whatever kind of seed you want to sow outdoors, the soil preparation is the same. Do it when the soil is moist but not sticky, and if you are proposing to sow the same day, choose a time when rain is forecast to follow shortly. The soil should be forked to the depth of the tines, and the lumps knocked down so that it is evenly broken up throughout, and all weeds and stones rigorously removed. Then it should be trodden evenly all over and raked again to break up the smooth surface and produce the crumb-like structure required for successful seed germination. Rake it twice, the second time at right angles to the first, and make sure it is level and firm. Hollows cause seed to be washed into patches by rain, so that seedlings are crowded; uneven firmness, with soft or hard soil alternating, will result in erratic germination and growth of seedlings.

The dappled shade provided by light woodland is ideal for shade-loving plants such as foxgloves and decorative foliage shrubs.

Table 5.1

Plants grown from seed outdoors:	*Less often grown:*
Vegetables	Shrubs
Annuals (flowering plants which live for less than a year)	Trees
Biennials (flower in their second year, then die)	Bulbs
Herbaceous perennials	Conifers
Rock plants	
Alpine strawberries	
Herbs	

Warm soil encourages rapid seed germination, so the period mid- to late spring is one of the best times to sow, when the air temperature is rising steadily and with it that of the soil. You can help Nature still further by putting cloches on the soil about two weeks before sowing. Early autumn is also good, though with the winter in prospect seedlings will need more care to get them through it.

If seed is being sown by scattering it all over the soil, as with flowering annuals or certain vegetables, wholesale soil preparation like this is essential. However, if you are short of time, it is possible to cheat by simply preparing the soil where rows are to be sown, as is often done for vegetables or flowers for cutting.

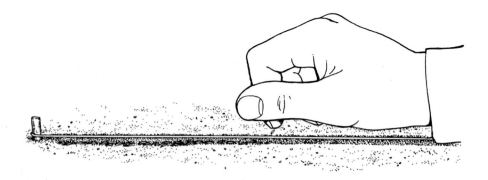

Fig. 8 Successful germination is ensured if seed is sown evenly and thinly in a drill, and the drill is evenly deep.

Sowing seeds in a row is done by making a small furrow in the soil with the corner of a hoe, along a string stretched tight just above the soil between two canes (Fig. 8). You can line this with moist potting compost for an even better start, then sow the seed thinly and evenly along the furrow, and cover it firmly with about 6 mm ($\frac{1}{4}$ in) depth of more compost or soil. To save seed you can 'station' sow, that is, sow a few seeds at intervals of 2.5 or 5 cm (1 or 2 in). Water with a fine-rose watering can, and protect from cats and birds with wire netting; cloches will keep them warm as well. Watering the drill before sowing will be a great help for good germination.

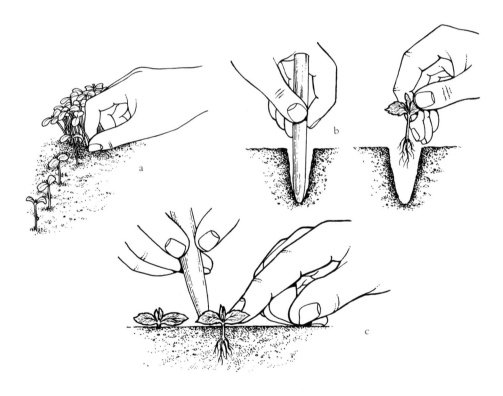

Fig. 9 (*a*) Seedlings are thinned for the first time when large enough to handle, at about the first true leaf stage. (*b*) When planting small plants, use a dibber to make a hole, but not in clay soils; for these use a trowel. (*c*) Put the plant in so that the stem is buried and the seed leaves only just above the soil surface.

AFTERCARE

As seeds will not germinate without moisture and oxygen, you will need to watch that the surface soil does not become dry. If rain is in short supply, water gently but thoroughly with a watering-can and fine rose attached. Germination takes one to three weeks for the majority of seeds, and the lower the temperature the longer it will take. If the spring is cold, they may rot in the ground, so cloches or plastic tunnels already in place will be doubly useful.

Once they germinate, spring-sown seeds can be thinned when large enough to handle, usually when they have two 'seed' leaves and one 'true' leaf (Fig. 9). Early thinning ensures strong plants later: leave about 2.5 cm (1 in) between them. For the second thinning, thin to their final spacing in most cases. Occasionally a third one is necessary. If station-sown, thin once, to the strongest at each station. After thinning, firm down the soil around the remaining seedlings and water to settle the soil still further.

Seeds sown in early autumn do not need thinning until the spring, but should be watched all the same. The autumn leaf-fall should be removed from seed-beds and rows, and an eye kept on the slugs and snails having a last meal before hibernating, otherwise there will not be any seedlings left in spring. Cloche protection in severe or prolonged cold is advisable.

SEED SOWING IN CONTAINERS

Sowing in seed containers is one of the ways of fighting off trouble with slugs and snails, especially when you are dealing with vegetables. Cell-trays (Fig. 10) are one of the most convenient types of container, in which the cells have a width of about 4 cm ($1\frac{1}{2}$ in), and depth of 5 cm (2 in). You can sow two or three seeds in the centre of each, thin to the strongest, and leave them there until four to six leaves are present, when they are in fact small plants. Then plant out, when it is unlikely that the mollusc population will eat them. They prefer seedlings and tiny plants. Presumably the flavour is sweeter, and the leaves more tender.

Other containers for seed are: small plastic pots 2.5 cm (1 in) diameter; Jiffy discs, dry compressed peat which swells when soaked to form a cylinder of peat about 3 × 5 cm ($1\frac{3}{4}$ × 2 in) contained by plastic mesh; plastic or wooden seed-trays 35 × 23 × 5/7.5 cm (14 × 9 × $\frac{2}{3}$ in); also half trays and quarter trays. The Jiffy 7s can be planted complete, which saves injury to the roots, as with the plants grown in cell-trays or small pots. This method also saves time, as there is no pricking-off to do, i.e. transplanting the seedlings into a tray at a wider spacing to wean them before planting them outdoors, or in a large container.

Fig. 10 Cell trays are convenient to carry and can also be used for pricking out seedlings, where they can be left to grow on.

COMPOST
A peat-based compost gives good germination, and there are several proprietary ones available which can be used for seed or potting. There is also the John Innes seed compost which contains soil as well as peat and sand. Both kinds are available from garden centres, chain stores and shops (see also p. 00)

CONTAINER PREPARATION
As with outdoor seed sowing, a level surface and even firmness are essential. When filling a tray, firm the corners and sides first, then the centre. Bang it gently on the work surface to level it, and then level and firm still further with a presser, a piece of board with a handle. When complete the container should have a space between the compost surface and lip of the container, to allow for watering. Then put the tray, or whatever container is being used, in a shallow tray of water and leave it to soak through the compost until the surface is dark and moist. Take out and leave to drain, then there should be no need to water again until germination occurs.

SOWING SEED
When sowing seed in the larger containers, sow it thinly and evenly all over the surface, or in lines, and cover with a fine layer of compost, to the depth of the seed. If it is fine and dust-like, do not cover at all. Then put a black plastic sheet over it, and keep in a suitable temperature for the variety. Keeping the temperature above the recommended minimum, and constant moisture, are the golden rules for container germination.

Fig. 11 Potting on
(*a*) A plant needs to be potted on when its roots reach the container sides and emerge from the drainage holes. (*b*) Remove by inverting the pot on to the palm of the hand and tapping the pot rim on the work surface. (*c*) Prepare the new, larger pot by filling in a little compost at the base, and use drainage crocks if the pot is clay. (*d*) Centre the soil ball and fill in until it is level with the top of the soil ball. The depth of compost should ensure that top of soil ball is 2.5 cm below pot rim.

AFTERCARE

Look at the seeds every day, especially when the day temperature is above 21°C (70°F), as some germinate very quickly at these high temperatures, within two or three days of sowing. If left covered, they rapidly become pale and leggy and permanently weak, and you will need to start again. After germination, the temperature can be gradually lowered; thin the seedlings as for outdoor seeds. Transplant and pot, if necessary, as they grow, until large enough to plant out. When potting, use a pot 2.5 cm (1 in) in diameter larger than the previous one, and always leave a space at the top of the pot for watering (Fig. 11). If grown indoors, accustom the young plants to outdoor temperatures gradually, by putting them in a frame or a sunny place by day, and bringing them in or closing the frame at night, until they can be left out or open all the time.

· CHAPTER 6 ·

WEATHER-WISE
GARDENING

The majority of people live in towns and cities nowadays, surrounded by rows of terraced houses, shops, tower blocks, and buildings of all sorts. The soil is covered with tarmac, paving or concrete, and there is very little left of plant life, except for what grows in gardens, which are nearly always small, and the occasional park, public garden or playing field. The warmth generated and maintained by these buildings is higher than it is in the countryside. Rain, frost, snow and drought are tempered by these surroundings and, because there is little sky to be seen, even the sunlight isn't the glory that it is in the rural landscape.

In particular, the wind is tamed most days to a degree that is barely noticeable, and it is highly unlikely that the average urbanite knows on any given day which direction it is coming from. In short, the weather in the city is 'muffled', and probably the only time it really makes its presence felt is when the traffic snarls up into impenetrable jams during heavy rain.

Nevertheless, the weather is still an important factor, and if you want to garden successfully as well as organically, it is essential to be aware of what it is doing all the time. Country gardeners are only too well aware of it, having sometimes to contend with snowdrifts, floods, drought, gales and extremes of temperature; town gardeners will experience all these things, though to a lesser degree, but with the added problem that somehow they are not obvious until some time after they begin, part of the 'muffling' effect.

If you don't watch the weather, the damage that can result is such that growing anything can be a complete waste of time. Late frosts in late spring and early summer can see off normally hardy seedlings and young plants as well as tender bedding plants. Night frost in midsummer is not unknown and can cause sprouting broccoli to 'sprout' at the end of late summer, as I know to my cost. Hail can ruin a crop of tomatoes; summer gales break branches, stems and flowers off flowering shrubs, runner beans and delphiniums; and drought will kill many plants outright and severely weaken those that do survive. By being aware in advance that all these catastrophes can occur, you can take steps to prevent them or to obviate them. As much as anything, success in avoiding them lies in

(*Left*) This gooseberry has been well mulched with rotted farm manure to keep the soil well fed and in good condition.

(*Opposite*) The weather can have a disastrous effect and the possibility of damage should always be kept in mind.

knowing that damage is feasible, and that the weather can be fierce, as well as unpredictable.

WEATHER FORECASTS

One of the two major aids to assessing what the weather will be like from day to day, and what its long term trends are is the weather forecast. The television forecasts are particulary helpful in showing the pattern of lows and highs in your area for the day in question, and the week's forecast, usually shown on Sundays, gives a very good idea of the trends, especially useful for frost forecasts, gales, and continuance or not of drought.

However, bear in mind that these forecasts need a little adjustment for your neighbourhood. For instance, rain may be forecast, but by the time the low concerned reaches your district, all the rain may have been shed, and this will be a pattern that happens regularly. It may be necessary to water certain plants after all, but if you are prepared for this, they will not be weakened and become infested with greenfly. With experience you can learn to interpret the forecasts in relation to your area, and you will also, if you have television or a daily newspaper, come to understand that certain combinations of anti-cyclones, warm fronts and low pressure systems will produce particular trends in the weather.

THE WIND

The other key to the weather, of more immediate help in your own area, is the wind, or lack of it, and its direction. Broadly speaking, wind from the south-west or west nearly always means that rain is on the way; a north, north-east or north-west wind brings cool or cold temperatures, clear sky and sun, but no rain. In winter a wind out of the north or north-

east means snow eventually. If the wind blows directly east in winter, protect everything and stay indoors. A south-east wind is a contradiction in terms as it blows from warm and cold regions at the same time, and the weather bears this out; be prepared for anything to happen with this wind: rain, a sea-fog (if you live near the coast), sun or thin cloud. A south wind is not necessarily hot, it can be quite chilly, but is unlikely to bring much rain, if any, though it can call up the odd thunderstorm.

Be aware of when the wind is increasing, and when it is dying down as either condition means a change in the weather, and watch the sky, too, for the high wind as it moves the clouds along. A particularly important wind effect in spring and again in mid-late autumn occurs when a day-time wind drops and dies away to nothing as darkness comes. If the sky is clear, or is clearing at the same time, be ready for a sudden and very sharp drop in temperature to produce a snap frost. This often happens so quickly that it is not forecast, and you really do need to know your local climate and be on the alert, so that plants can be protected.

DAILY RECORDS

If you can spare the time, and it doesn't take long, keeping a daily record of the weather through the year for several years is an enormous help in determining the trends likely at a particular season. You need not do more than note the rain, sun, a rough idea of the temperature, e.g. cool, warm, hot, etc., snow, mist, the minimum night temperature, and the wind direction and strength, and you will find that, in spite of the apparent vagaries of the weather, there are distinct patterns at particular times of the year. You will be able to see when the temperature begins to rise in spring, and the point at which it becomes neccessary to take precautions against cold in autumn, the times when gales are most likely, and the periods at which irrigation becomes important.

MICRO-CLIMATES

As you become experienced in assessing the weather for your region, so it is important to notice what goes on in the enclosed area of the garden. Within this there will be several different micro-climates, and if you adjust the type of plants you grow in them accordingly, again you will have stronger and better plants, naturally growing more healthily, and less likely to need the crutches of artificial fertilizers, and the medicines of sprays and powders.

One of the more common micro-climates is a frost-pocket, an area of the garden where frost lingers well into midday when all other parts have thawed. Cold air sinks to the lowest point and then builds up deeper and deeper, like water, if there is no outlet. A fence with a gap under it will let it through; a garden on a slope should be free unless there are sites where plants and shrubs form a thicket round a bed to contain the cold air in it.

A wind-tunnel between house and garage walls or between hedges is another micro-climate; an arbour facing south can be a hot sun-trap; and even within the confines of a raised bed there can be a micro-climate, of warmth and shelter quite distinct from the rest of the garden. If you can determine the areas in which these climate differences occur, you will have another tool to help you grow better plants, since you can then accurately fit the plants to the place.

GARDENING WITH THE WEATHER

In time, you can follow the general principle of choosing the right weather conditions for the job in hand. Establishing a new plant will be that much more successful if it is planted when rain is likely to follow soon after planting, but no frost, drought or gales. Tender bedding plants whose natural climate is a tropical one will survive if planted after frosts are likely, i.e. during early summer when the night temperature does not fall below 10°C (50°F), or is, hopefully, above 16°C (60°F).

Seed germination is much more certain with a rising soil temperature, soil already moistened by rain and rain likely to follow soon after sowing. Digging in late autumn or early winter gets the job done while the soil is still malleable and leaves it rough for the frost to work on it, and cuts down your own labour the following spring. Mulching after rain, instead of before it, keeps the soil moist, saves work, and helps the plants.

You can use the weather to help you garden organically, even if you can only garden at weekends. It can be a tool to be worked with, rather than a weapon to be fought against, so that the plants and the garden thrive because of it, not in spite of it.

CHAPTER 7

VEGETABLE HUSBANDRY

Growing vegetables in Victorian times was reminiscent of Mrs. Beeton's cookery: where she would say 'take a quart of cream and a dozen eggs', as a matter of course, the Victorian head gardener would advise taking 'a load of dung and a barrowful of loam from the nearest field'. The days when such farm manure was to be had for the taking disappeared with the First World War, and few gardeners now own a sufficiently large garden to include a field, even if the labour is available to dig out the loam.

With such a start, it was difficult not to grow strong, vigorous vegetables. The soil was maintained in superb condition with annual dressings of rotted organic matter, and the vegetables responded to it in yield, taste and health. However, there is no reason why modern vegetable growers should not obtain the same results, by following the soil management discussed in Chapter 3, supplemented with a variety of cultural practices aimed at dispensing as far as possible with the need to use pesticide controls and weedkillers.

SEED SELECTION

One of the most obvious of these is the choice of seed. A great deal of plant breeding has been done in the last 30 years and this has resulted in greatly improved crops for a variety of reasons. Yields are up on the old pre-war ones; the cropping time is often quicker; smaller varieties are available, making it easier for the gardener to fit a greater choice into the garden and, the biggest benefit of all, resistance to disease and in some cases to pests, has been bred into the new varieties. The resistance may only be partial to, say canker in parsnips, or leafmould on tomatoes, but even a little is better than nothing. This fact will always be mentioned in the seedsman's description of the vegetable, so whenever you can, look for and choose a resistant variety.

For an even better start, obtain seed and/or plants from an organic grower; it should have a strong constitution and resistance built into it from the way in which it was produced, thus giving it an inherent ability to overcome any environmental problems.

ROTATION

A second outstanding cultural practice, still surviving from the last century, is that of rotation of the crops. Plans for rotating can be many and complicated, with permutations and combinations worthy of the football pools, but basically the essence of rotation is 'don't plant a crop in the same place two years running'. By doing this, you prevent the establishment and increase of a particular disease or pest in the soil, and you avoid the occurrence of a nutrient shortage, brought on by a vegetable which needs a particular mineral or minerals. Originally rotation was instituted to prevent clubroot of cabbages infecting the soil. Unfortunately, there is no cure for it, it lasts for many years in the soil and plants are killed by it, so it was a disaster when it appeared. All the cabbage family are prone to infection and it was quite possible for the whole of the kitchen garden soil to become contaminated.

To make rotation simpler, vegetables can be divided into three groups: the cabbage family; the root crops; and potatoes together with peas and beans. These divisions take account of the organic matter and food needs of the plants, too, since cabbages and their relatives do best on soil dressed with organic matter the previous autumn, and limed in winter; root crops should follow another crop which grew in manure-treated soil the previous season, and potatoes do best on soil containing organic matter worked in shortly before planting, as do the legumes. A further refinement for the root crops is that lime should not be used, but they do like potash, so wood ashes or rock potash should be mixed in.

Table 7.1 Crop rotation

1st year		
cabbage, Brussels sprouts, cauliflower, sprouting broccoli, calabrese, kohl rabi, kale, pak choi, pe tsai, lettuce, spinach, Swiss chard	carrots, parsnip, radish, turnip, beetroot, swede, celeriac, scorzonera, salsify, Hamburg parsley, tomatoes	potatoes, peas, beans of all kinds, onions, shallots, leeks, cucumbers, marrows, courgette, celery
A	B	C
2nd year		
B	C	A
3rd year		
C	A	B

You can vary this a little, for instance early carrots or beet could fill in the spaces waiting for the brassicas, and if you want maincrop carrots to be sown late in early summer, lettuce or broad beans could fill the space in spring. Crops like asparagus and globe artichokes, being permanent, do not form part of a rotation. Jerusalem artichokes will grow in most soils and make a good wind protection. But whatever you do, follow the principle of planting different successive crops in one site, even if it is a case of only moving a row or two away.

COMPANION PLANTING

If you have the space, you could try experimenting with companion planting. Some vegetables, grown in association with others, are thought to grow better, and to be kept free from pest infestation, for instance lettuce associate well with cucumbers, and potatoes do well with peas. The converse applies in that cabbages grow badly if planted close to onions, and red cabbage should not be a neighbour of tomatoes. This is a complicated subject, but well worth pursuing. For more information see p. 94.

PEST EVASION

When it comes to the actual time of sowing or planting, it is worth remembering that the life cycles of many pests are geared to ensuring that the larvae have plenty of food of the right sort conveniently to hand the instant they hatch. Hence many of them hatch just when, for instance, carrot roots are in their most succulent youth, cabbage leaves are tender and increasing in number, lettuce seedlings have just germinated, and there is a plentiful supply of young Brussels sprout roots.

The time at which most vegetables are sown is mid-spring, but if you can sow earlier and protect, or sow much later in early summer, you stand a good chance of avoiding damage from many pests, particularly carrot and onion root fly, and pea maggot. With good watering and thinning, you will still obtain maincrop carrots, if a quick-maturing variety is sown late in early summer. Onions sown late in May will not be as big as those sown in early or mid spring, but the damage saving will offset this. Alternatively, for onion-fly, use onion sets in mid spring — they will not be touched. Early peas sown late in winter or a late variety put in late in early summer, will mature when pea moth maggots are not about.

All this could presuppose a knowledge of all the life cycles of all the pests likely to infest vegetables, and there are books available which detail them, but in practice this information is not essential, though it can be useful. Sowing early and late, as suggested, is a help; good soil structure, ample plant food and water, care of the plants when young and use of resistant varieties, together with avoidance of inorganic sprays throughout the garden, will ensure that little damage occurs and that most of the insect pests are seen off by their predators in any case.

SPACING

Everything needs a minimum space in which to develop. Case studies of rats prove the point that in unacceptably crowded conditions they cease to breed and start to fight. If vegetables are not allowed the space they need for good growth, they also fight, but for moisture, air and food. If they are left too close together after planting or thinning, they will be starved, unhealthy and small, and inevitably will become badly infestd with pests, while disease will be able to spread to epidemic proportions.

Of course, with too much space between individual plants and rows the yields can be reduced. The mean between the two extremes is a fine one, but in general recent research and trials have found that spacing can be closer than used to be recommended.

The following is a list of suitable spacings for vegetables, which will make maximum use of space when grown in rows, without depleting the yield. It may need adjustment in the light of experience of your own soil and garden conditions, but it will form a basis from which to work.

Table 7.2 Vegetable spacings

Variety	Distance between plants and rows	
	(cm)	(in)
Artichoke, Jerusalem	35	15
Artichoke, globe	90–120	36–48
Asparagus	38 × 38	15 × 15
Beetroot, maincrop	15 × 30	6 × 12
Beetroot, early	7.5 × 20	3 × 8
Bean, broad, dwarf	23 × 23	9 × 9
Bean, broad, standard	12.5 × 45	5 × 18
Bean, runner	15 × 60	6 × 24
Bean, French	15 × 45	6 × 18
Brussels sprouts, dwarf	60 × 60	24 × 24
Brussels sprouts, standard	90 × 90	36 × 36
Carrot, early	2.5 × 5	1 × 2
Carrot, maincrop	5 × 15	2 × 6
Cabbage, spring	23 × 23	9 × 9

Variety	Distance between plants and rows	
	(cm)	(in)
Cabbage, summer and red	30 × 30	12 × 12
Cabbage, winter and white	38 × 38	15 × 15
Cabbage, savoy	45 × 45	18 × 18
Cabbage, chinese	30 × 38	12 × 15
Cauliflower, summer	50 × 50	20 × 20
Cauliflower, winter	75 × 75	30 × 30
Cucumber, trailing	75 × 75	30 × 30
Cucumber, climbing	45 × 45	18 × 18
Celeriac	30 × 38	12 × 15
Celery, summer	27.5 × 27.5	11 × 11
Celery, winter	30 × 38	12 × 15
Chicory	15–23 × 15–23	6–9 × 6–9
Endive	30 × 30	12 × 12
Kohl rabi	10 × 30	4 × 12
Leek	10–15 × 30	4–6 × 12
Lettuce, cabbage	23–30 × 25	9–12 × 10
Lettuce, cabbage, small, and cos	15 × 23	6 × 9
Marrow	180 × 90	72 × 36
Onion	10 × 25	4 × 10
Onion, pickling	patch-sow, do not thin	
Onion, spring	20 cm (8 in), do not thin	
Parsnip	10–15 × 20–30	4–6 × 8–12
Pea	2 × times ht. of cultivar	5
Potato, early	25 × 38	10 × 15
Potato, maincrop	30–38 × 75	12–15 × 30
Radish, summer	2.5 × 10	1 × 4
Radish, winter	15 × 30	6 × 12
Salsify, scorzonera	15 × 30	6 × 12
Shallots	10 × 23	4 × 9
Spinach, summer	30 × 30	12 × 12
Spinach, winter	20 × 30	8 × 12
Spinach, perpetual	30 × 38	12 × 15
Sprouting broccoli	60 × 60	24 × 24
Swede	23 × 38	9 × 15
Sweetcorn	30–38 × 30–38	12–15 × 12–15
Swiss chard	30 × 38	12 × 15
Tomato	38 × 60	15 × 24
Turnip, early	10 × 23	4 × 9
Turnip, maincrop	20 × 30	8 × 12

WATERING

One of the most important cultural practices for getting healthy, heavy yielding vegetables is maintaining the supply of water. Vegetables consist of at least 80% water – marrows and cucumbers are more than 90% – and they need a steady supply the whole time they are growing. Root crops are particularly vulnerable, especially when young, from the thinning stage to about halfway through their life, but it is better not to make exceptions, and to assume that all need plenty of water all the time.

Table 7.3 Watering requirements for vegetables

Vegetables	Quantity of water	Time and frequency
Root crops	5 l/sq m (1 gal/sq yd) when young 18 l/sq m ($3\frac{1}{2}$ gal/sq yd) while maturing	in dry weather every two weeks
Potatoes, earlies maincrops	18 l/sq m ($3\frac{1}{2}$ gal/sq yd) 22 l/sq m ($4\frac{1}{2}$ gal/sq yd)	every two weeks once, at flowering time
Onions	5 l/sq m (1 gal/sq yd)	every two weeks in dry weather from late spring to early in midsummer
Peas/beans	7.5 l/sq m ($1\frac{1}{2}$ gal/sq yd)	every two weeks from flowering
Marrows/cucumbers	4.5 l (1 gal) per plant	from final planting, once a week
Aubergines/peppers/sweetcorn outdoors	4.5 l (1 gal) per plant	every week from flowering
Tomatoes outdoors	4.5 l (1 gal) per plant	every three to four days from flowering
Leaf and stem vegetables including kohl rabi (not Brussels sprouts unless weather very dry)	11 l/sq m ($2\frac{1}{2}$ gal/sq yd)	every week
Transplants in summer	0.14 l ($\frac{1}{4}$ pt) per plant	daily until growing well

A typical lush and healthy vegetable garden which can be obtained by using organic methods of gardening.

If you have a heavy but well broken-down soil with a clay subsoil, the water reserves will be good, even in drought. A medium loam or a sandy, stony or chalky soil will need a lot of watering unless there is a good deal of heavy rain throughout the season, following a wet or snowy winter. Mulching on to moist soil in spring is a great help, and if it contains organic matter, so much the better, as this acts like a sponge. Although it sounds like heresy, a light weed cover can protect the soil from surface drying under hot sun, but it should be hoed off before flowering starts. Strips of old carpet or matting can be used as a mulch along rows or round plants to contain the moisture if organic mulches are few and far between.

Actual watering, even in a season of average rainfall, can make a great deal of difference to the final yields, as well as the establishment of young transplants, many of which are moved at a time when the weather is likely to be at its hottest and driest, early – midsummer. It will be vital in dry periods, and even when the season's total rainfall is higher than usual, there may still be crucial stages in a crop's life when rain is temporarily absent. As a general guide the quantities shown in Table 7.3 can be used, but as with spacing, they can be tailored to each crop for maximum yield and flavour in the light of experience of your soil and local rainfall.

FEEDING

Provided the soil is being correctly treated in the first place (see Chapter 3), it will contain a quantity of plant foods supplied from both organic matter and from the concentrated fertilizers added when preparing it for sowing or planting. Supplementing these supplies while vegetables are growing may be necessary in some cases, in some seasons and in certain soils, particularly the quick-draining kinds. If so, use the more quickly acting fertilizers, and use them in solution if possible, otherwise water in directly after application.

Be guided by the manufacturers' instructions for rates and frequencies of application but, if in doubt, use half the quantities of dry fertilizers recommended for pre-planting/sowing dressings, halfway through the season, or use solutions once a week. Liquid seaweed is excellent, such as Maxicrop or Chase SM3. You can make up your own liquid fertilizer with a sack of farm manure suspended in a barrel of water until the liquid is dark-coloured, then use by diluting to a pale biscuit colour. Comfrey leaves in water provide a solution high in potassium, as well as containing nitrogen and phosphorus; use 0.75 kg ($1\frac{1}{2}$ lb) to 11 l ($2\frac{1}{2}$ gal) of water, and dilute the solution on a 1 : 1 basis. Use either in place of a normal watering about once a week.

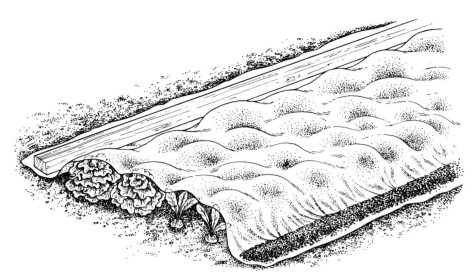

Fig. 12 A 'floating' cloche is made of synthetic fibre fleece, which keeps seedlings warm, protects from wind and allows rain through.

PROTECTING CROPS

Crops need two kinds of protection: that which prevents them from being damaged by extremes of weather, and that which keeps birds and small mammals from attacking them. The latter will be dealt with in Chapter 10 where specific treatment of pests and diseases is discussed. Problems caused by the weather can usually be circumvented by one means or another, and it is not often that it is necessary to give it best. Some weather conditions physically harm the plants, others have an indirect and long-term effect.

WIND AND GALES
Can tear and brown leaves and flowers of climbers in particular, such as runner beans and climbing French beans, marrows and cucumbers grown up wire netting and vegetables in general. Use wind barriers such as fences, hedges, Jerusalem artichokes, panels of plastic glazing or commercial windbreak netting – ask your local garden centre about the last-named. Support Brussels sprouts and sprouting broccoli with stout 90-cm (3-ft) stakes in late summer.

DROUGHT
For protection from drying out, see pp.54–56. Steady moisture supplies will prevent splitting and cracking of fruit and root vegetables, and dropping of flowers.

An excellent crop of onions grown from sets which are not attacked by onion fly and therefore need no spraying.

LOW TEMPERATURES
In spring, use cloches, plastic tunnels, plastic bottles with the base removed, tents made of plastic sheet (Fig. 12), Agryl fleece or Hortopaper, to cover seedlings and small plants at night. Agryl and Hortopaper can be stretched completely over a seedbed. Where practicable cover the soil in advance with any of these to prevent frost reaching it. In autumn cover summer sowings of lettuce, Chinese cabbage, vegetable fennel, carrots, beet, bush tomatoes, the last cucumbers and New Zealand spinach, to keep up the night temperature particularly, as long as possible. In winter keep lettuce, perpetual spinach, parsley, chicory and any root crops still in the ground, covered with cloches or tunnels against snow and frost.

HEAVY RAIN
Grow vegetables in raised beds; dig temporary drainage channels leading away from the site; dig coarse grit into heavy soil when preparing it, at 3 kg/sq m (7 lb/sq yd). Ensure that any bare soil surface has an organic mulch on it to prevent 'capping', when the surface becomes smooth, hard and unbroken under the continual pounding of heavy rain.

HAIL
Can ruin the fruiting crops such as tomatoes, aubergines, cucumbers, courgette, and peppers to a lesser degree. If you have time, cover vegetables at once with plastic sheet. Heavy gauge plastic sacks opened out are useful.

HIGH TEMPERATURES
As for drought. Maintain soil moisture at all times and spray overhead several times a day, as this prevents excess transpiration of moisture from leaves and stems, which can lead to leaf-tipburn.

CHAPTER 8

THE FRUITFUL GARDEN

Growing one's own fruit organically pays almost more than it does to grow organic vegetables, because most commercially-grown fruit is sprayed with at least one chemical nearly every week, from early spring to near harvest, particularly apples and pears. All those used by commercial growers are approved by the Ministry of Agriculture, but chemical controls for fruit pests and diseases have only been in use for about 25 years and, after DDT, no one can be justified in categorically stating that any of those in current use will not have the same catastrophic results.

THE START

When choosing your fruit varieties, look for those which are guaranteed 'Certified Stock'. The Ministry of Agriculture runs certification schemes for certain varieties of fruit, not all of them, and these schemes cover apples and pears, strawberries, raspberries, blackcurrants and blackberries, hybrid berries, gooseberries, cherries and plums. There are two grades of certified stock: the 'A' grade is the easiest to obtain, and indicates that the plants are strong, healthy and free from a variety of diseases, depending on the fruit concerned. This is particularly useful for raspberries and strawberries, which used to be badly infested with virus diseases such as mosaic and yellows; for apples, in which rubbery wood virus was a common problem in 'Lord Lambourne'; and for pears, which carried stony pit virus.

Fruit trees and bushes can become infested with a great variety of pests and diseases which spoil the appearance of the individual fruits, cause rotting, reduce the yield and stunt growth. It is even more important to start this type of plant well, as nearly all of them are permanent, long term providers. If you attempt to remedy a poor start several years afterwards, it is rarely successful, and the weak plants which result will always be prone to bad infestations.

PREPARING SOIL

Soil preparation should therefore never be skimped; dig it well, clean it thoroughly of weeds and lace it with bulky organics which are thoroughly rotted. The most suitable soils for fruit are deep, at least 30 cm (12 in), preferably 60 cm (24 in), and well-drained, with a slightly acid reaction, and good water reserves in the subsoil. Attempting to grow fruit organically in shallow alkaline soil over a chalk subsoil represents such a challenge that it is best avoided unless you have no alternative and are a dedicated fruit enthusiast. If the soil is sandy or stony, mix in a balanced compound fertilizer as well as rotted organic matter, e.g. organic Growmore about 10 days before planting, at the rate recommended by the makers.

PLANTING

The best season for planting fruit is still late autumn, with early winter a close second, while the soil is warm, but not yet saturated or frozen, and when the trees or bushes are winding down for winter dormancy. Whether you use container grown or bare root plants can depend on price, convenience and accessibility but, given a choice, I would prefer bare roots, so that they can be spread out naturally in the planting hole, and develop without the preliminary kinking and cramping associated with container-grown plants.

STAKING

Supports are important for all fruit except strawberries, and bush forms of currants and gooseberries. Bush, standard and half-standard forms of tree fruits need a single slanting stake, or a double one with a cross-bar, rammed well into the planting hole before siting the tree, which should be about 15 cm (6 in) from the stake, attached to it with tree ties or old nylon tights. The stake's top should reach to just below the tree's head.

Soft fruit, that is, raspberries, loganberries and similar cane fruits and restricted forms of redcurrants and gooseberries, together with top fruit such as cordons, fans and espaliers, will need a support system of wires and posts, or wires attached to fences or walls. Posts need to be well rammed in to a depth of at least 30 cm (1 ft), preferably 45 cm ($1\frac{1}{2}$ ft), and height above soil should be 150–180 cm (5–6 ft). Fans and espaliers do best with a wall or fence support 180–210 cm (6–7 ft) high, which also supplies warmth and protection from wind. The main branches of both these forms, together with cordons, need to be trained and tied to single canes to keep them straight and pointing in the required directions at the correct angle.

SPACING

As with vegetables, the right spacing is important, particularly as many fruits are prone to rotting because of fungus disease infection. Strawberries and raspberries rot rapidly with grey mould if stools or crowns are planted close together; brown rot can be a big problem on plums, apples and pears, and mildew can be devastating on gooseberries. In crowded plantings, the air is humid and undisturbed, an ideal condition for the spread of fungus spores from fruit to fruit, but if spaced correctly so that there is good air circulation between the plants, and all parts receive light and the sun's warmth, fungus diseases either do not appear or have difficulty in spreading. The table given on pp. 68–69 details spacings for individual fruits.

CARE WHEN ESTABLISHED

Once the fruit is planted, it will need more or less maintenance, depending on the variety, but on the whole fruit cultivation is not as time-consuming as that of vegetables. Pest and disease control would normally take up a good deal of time, but organically-grown fruit will hardly be troubled in this respect, so that jobs to be done are basically standard cultural practices which ensure that the plants have a regular supply of food and water, that the soil structure continues to be good, and that the growth is controlled to obtain a balance between crop and shoot/leaf development.

FEEDING

The average soil will already contain plant foods to some degree. More will have been added at planting, and some will be returned at leaf fall, but the removal of the fruit means that part of the nutrients is lost permanently from the soil. This will be replaced to some extent by regular mulching with rotted organic matter, and in some soils this is all that need be done, particularly in heavy soil which has already been well worked for some years and is well broken down. But for the first few years at least, regular feeding with the organic form of Growmore already mentioned, is advisable, applied at the end of late winter and watered in if no rain (or snow!) occurs. This sounds early, but tree roots will already be coming to life again, and organic fertilizers take time to be absorbed into the soil and become available to plant roots.

Alternatively blood-fish-and-bone can be used, and should be forked carefully into the top few cm (in) of soil. Gooseberries and redcurrants have a need for potash, and the ashes resulting from burning prunings can be used at the same time, at about 120 g/sq m (4 oz/sq yd). They can contain 7% potash; calcium will also be present, and it is perhaps better for alkaline soils if the ashes are mixed into the compost heap. The stone fruits need calcium, and if growing in acid soil, should have 250 g/sq m (8 oz/sq yd) ground chalk added every few years, early in the winter.

Straw is still one of the best materials for mulching strawberries.

Summer-fruiting strawberries begin to make their new fruiting crowns for the following season in the summer, when they have finished fruiting, and half the fertilizer dressing can be added at that time, when cleaning up the plants and freeing them from weeds and excess runners.

WATERING
The soft fruits are shallow rooting, with thin fibrous roots, and are particularly vulnerable to water shortages, especially when they are producing new growth at the same time as cropping. Lack of water not only stunts this new growth, on which next season's fruit will be formed, but causes the fruit to be hard, small and flavourless. In dry hot weather keep them well watered, especially raspberries and strawberries; give raspberries about 22 l/sq m (4$\frac{1}{2}$ gal/sq yd) as the berries start to swell, and water strawberries at about 5 l/sq m (1 gal/sq yd) whenever required between late spring and late summer.

Top fruit usually only requires watering if grown against a wall or fence, and in dry summer weather should be given about 22 l/sq m (4$\frac{1}{2}$ gal/sq yd) every 7–10 days.

MULCHING
This is essential for all fruit and should always consist of organic matter.

Covering the soil with a black plastic sheet is often suggested for straw-berries, but this can provide a good hiding place in daytime for slugs and snails after they have fed on the berries at night, and straw is better.

Put the mulch on in spring, when the soil is moist and free of weeds; thickness can be 5–10 cm(2–4 in) and should cover the area over which the roots extend, which will be at least to the same distance that the top growth extends above the soil. Use any of the materials described in Chapter 3. Summer-fruiting strawberries can have an additional light mulch put on after cropping in late summer.

PRUNING

Left to themselves, fruit trees and bushes will grow into a wild tangle of disorganized branches and shoots with only a few poor-sized fruit on them, generally badly damaged by pests and birds. Pruning helps to control the vegetative growth so that there is a great deal less of it, and a consequent increase in crop, thus balancing the shoot/fruit ratio. However, the pruning has to be done at the right time of the year, and it has to remove the right growth, otherwise the shoots which are going to carry fruit the following year are cut off – this is one of the many reasons for a poor fruit crop.

By controlling growth, you enable light, warmth and air to reach all parts of the tree or bush to mature the growth and ripen the crop evenly; good ventilation cuts down the spread of disease and pests, and energy is channelled into fruit production rather than just shoot growth.

There are one or two points to remember that make all the difference between right and wrong pruning. One is that the new season's shoots are green and soft until late in the summer, when the bark gradually begins to turn brown from the base of the shoot upwards; in succeeding years the bark is hard and the shoot or branch stiff and rigid. A second is that fruit buds on fruit trees are fat and rounded; vegetative buds which are going to produce leaves and new shoots are long, thin and narrow. A third is that some fruit crops on shoots newly produced the previous season; other fruit varieties crop on two-year-old and older shoots. For example, blackcurrants produce a heavy crop on one-year-old shoots, but redcurrants will not do so until the shoots are in their second sum-mer, consequently the pruning for the two has to be quite different.

When making the pruning cuts, use a good sharp pair of secateurs or a knife, so that no ragged edges are left, and place the cut so that it is just above a bud or leaf – if a snag is left it is likely to become diseased. Slant the cut away from the bud, so that rain does not run down on to it.

Table 8.1 gives a brief description of pruning the different sorts of fruit, and the time of year to do it.

Table 8.1 Pruning

Variety	Time of year	Method
Apple, bush	winter	Cut back sideshoots which have carried fruit to a stub 5 or 7.5 cm (2 or 3 in) long; treat one third of the sideshoots back each year. Cut leading shoots back by about a quarter to one third.
Apple, cordon and espalier	late in mid summer, winter, spring	Cut sideshoots back to the 4th leaf above the basal cluster when the bark of the shoot is beginning to turn brown, but the tip is still soft and green; cut them back again to 1 bud in winter. Allow leading shoot to grow until space filled, then cut to maintain this in late spring each year.
Blackberry, loganberry, hybrid berries	after fruiting	Cut fruited shoots down to ground level; tie new ones in their place, evenly spaced; do not retain weak new canes.
Blackcurrant	after fruiting or in late autumn – early winter	Cut fruited shoots either down to ground level, or back to strong new shoot.
Cherry, sweet, fan form	summer, autumn	Remove the tip of each sideshoot when the fifth leaf has developed; cut back further in early autumn to just above the third bud; cut leading shoots to fit their space.
Cherry, acid, fan form	summer	Thin out sideshoots as they form to allow space of 7.5 cm (3 in) between them and tie them in; in autumn cut out the fruited shoots, and retie the others for even spacing if necessary; cut leading shoots to fit their space.
Gooseberry★	early summer, late autumn	Cut back sideshoots to 5th leaf, and cut again in autumn to 2–3 buds. Cut leading shoots in autumn to leave half the new growth.

Peach, fan form	summer, autumn	Rub out all sideshoots when tiny, except for one at the base of each fruiting shoot and one halfway along it; tie these in as they grow, spacing them evenly; cut leading shoots back hard when they fill their space. In early autumn, cut fruited shoots out completely, and retie and space the remainder if necessary. Use the new shoot halfway along the fruited shoot if the basal new shoot did not develop.
Pear, bush, cordon, espalier	in the middle of mid-summer, winter	Cut sideshoots back as for apples at same stage of maturity, to 4th leaf, not counting basal cluster; cut again in winter to leave one bud. Cut leaders back when they have filled the space available to keep this filled.
Plum, bush	spring, late summer	Remove crowded, crossing, dead or damaged shoots. On older trees occasionally cut out a branch in spring and paint wound at once with protective compound.
Plum, fan form	summer, autumn	Pinch new sideshoots back when they have 6 leaves and tie in spaced at 10 cm (4 in) apart; remove any that are crowded. Immediately after fruiting cut these shoots back further, to 3 leaves. Cut out strong upright shoots completely.
Raspberry, summer fruiting	late summer	Cut all old fruited canes down to ground level; tie in new canes evenly spaced, remove all except the strongest, to a maximum of 6–8. In late winter cut the tips back by about 15 cm (6 in).
Raspberry, autumn fruiting	spring	As for summer fruiting kinds, but do not cut back tips of new canes.
Redcurrants	early summer, late autumn	Cut back sideshoots to 5th leaf; cut again in autumn to 1 bud. Cut leading shoots in autumn to leave 5–7.5 cm (2–3 in) new growth.
Strawberry		no formal pruning necessary, but remove unwanted runners as they appear.

*see note on birds on p. 81

PESTS AND DISEASES

Whole books have been written about the diseases of fruit, and also their pests, but they are mainly for the professional grower, and cover every conceivable problem that might affect fruit. For the gardener who grows only a few bushes and trees, there are not many diseases likely to be of concern, and even these will largely be kept under control by natural enemies in the unsprayed garden. Tips on treatment of the most likely troubles will be found in Chapter 10.

Table 8.2 Varieties for flavour

Apple (dessert)	*Blackcurrant*	*Loganberry*
Ashmead's Kernel	Ben Lomond	Loganberry L654
Cox Orange Pippin	Ben More	
D'Arcy Spice	Boskoop Giant	*Peach and Nectarine*
Discovery	Wellington	Bellegarde
Egremont Russet	Westwick Choice	Duke of York
Epicure		Lord Napier (nec.)
Fortune	*Cherry*	Peregrine
Greensleeves	Merton Bigarreau★	Pine Apple (nec.)
James Grieve	Merton Glory★	
Jonagold	Merchant★	*Pear* (dessert and
Lord Lambourne	Morello (acid)	culinary)
Orleans Reinette		Beurré Superfin
Queen Cox	*Damson*	Conference
Ribston Pippin	Bradley's King	Doyenné du Comice
Spartan	Merryweather	Williams' Bon Chrétien
Sunset	Shropshire Damson	Catillac (cul.)
	Gooseberry	*Plum*
Apple (culinary)	Crown Bob	Czar
Blenheim Orange	Invicta	Kirke's Blue
Bramley's Seedling	Jubilee	Marjorie's Seedling
Crawley Beauty	Lancashire Lad	Severn Cross
Howgate Beauty	Whinham's Industry	Utility
Norfolk Beauty	Whitesmith	Victoria
Blackberry	*Greengage*	*Raspberry*
Ashton Cross	Cambridge Gage	Autumn Bliss
Black Satin	Early Transparent	Glen Clova
Fantasia	Laxton Gage	Leo
John Innes	Late Transparent	Malling Admiral
Oregon Thornless	Pershore Yellow (jam)	Malling Jewel

Alpine strawberries and cordon apples do well together, with annual applications of rotted organic matter and slow-acting organic fertilizer.

Redcurrant	Strawberry (summer)	Strawberry (perpetual fruiting)
Jonkheer van Tets	Cambridge Vigour	Aromel
Rondom	Domanil	Gento
Redstart	Hapil	Rapello
White Versailles (white)	Tamella	

*needs pollinator. Morello will pollinate all and is self-fertile

Table 8.3 Quick-reference table of vital statistics for fruit

Variety	Preferred soil type	Rootstocks	Spacing m (ft)	Main harvest period	Yield per plant kg (lb)
Apple	deep, moist, medium to heavy	M26, dwarfing; M106, semi-dwarfing; M27, very dwarfing, needs fertile soil	bush 3–4.5 (10–15); cordon 0.6 (2); espalier 3.6 (12)	early–mid autumn	bush 23 (50); cordon 1.5–2.5 (3–5); espalier 9–13.5 (20–30)
Blackberry	moist, medium to heavy	own roots	3 × 1.8 (10 × 6)	early–mid autumn	4.5–11 (10–25)
Blackcurrant	moist, well-drained, medium to heavy	own roots	1.3 (4.5) each way	midsummer	4.5–7 (10–15)
Cherry, sweet (fan)	well-drained, deep, medium loam, neutral–slightly acid	'Colt'; dwarfing 'Pixie'	4.5 (15) on 'Colt'; 3 (10) on 'Pixie'	mid–late summer	9–18 (20–40) depending on stock
Cherry, acid (fan)	as sweet cherries	as sweet cherries	3.6 (12) on 'Colt'; 2.4 (8) on 'Pixie'	late summer–early autumn	4.5–6.5 (10–15)
Gooseberry	medium, well-drained, not wet or stony	own roots	1.4–1.8 (5–6)	early–midsummer	4.5–6.5 (10–15)
Loganberry	deep, well-drained, medium-heavy	own roots	2.4–3.6 (8–12)	mid–late summer	7 (15)
Peach, fan	heavy-medium, deep, well-drained	semi-vigorous 'St Julien A' and 'Mussel'; dwarfing 'Pixie'	4.5 (15); on 'Pixie' 3.6 (12)	late summer–early autumn	7–11.5 (15–25) depending on stock

Pear	deep, moist, well-drained, on the heavy side	semi-vigorous 'Quince A'; semi-dwarfing 'Quince C'	bush, espalier 3–4.5 (10–15); cordon 0.6–0.7 (2–2.5)	autumn	bush 14–18 (30–40); espalier 9–14 (20–30); cordon 2.5–2.7 (5–6)
Plum, bush	deep, moist, heavy, well-drained	semi-vigorous 'St Julien A'; dwarfing 'Pixie'	2.4–3.6 (8–12) on 'St Julien A'; on 'Pixie' 2.4 (8)	early autumn	22.5–45 (50–100), depending on stock and age
Plum, fan	as for bush	as for bush	3–4.5 (10–15) depending on stock	as bush	7–9 (15–20) depending on stock
Raspberry	medium-light, well-drained, organic matter important	own roots	45 cm (18 in) between plants; 1.5 (5) between rows	mid-late summer	0.7 (1.5) /30 cm (1 ft); autumn-fruiting 0.2 (0.5)
Redcurrant	medium, well-drained; add extra organic matter if light	own roots	1.5 (5)	midsummer	4.5–7 (10–15)
Strawberry	medium-light, well-drained, slightly acid to slightly alkaline	own roots	38 × 90 cm (15 × 36 in)	late-midsummer	0.2–0.5 (0.5–1); 56 g (2 oz) for alpine types

CHAPTER 9

GARDEN FLOWERS

Gardens by their very nature should be ornamental, and the largest part of most gardens is devoted to plants grown purely for beauty of the flowers and leaves; vegetables occupy perhaps one-tenth, fruit a smaller part, and protected plants even less. Herbs, if grown at all, may be only half a dozen. So the purely aesthetic aspect will dominate the garden and, because of this, can make or break success when growing crops organically. If organic principles are not followed in the ornamental parts of the garden, it will not be possible to grow vegetables or fruit organically either.

DIVERSITY

There are hundreds and hundreds of plants for decoration, and if you can grow as many different kinds as possible, you will ensure that you have a vast range of insects of all kinds also inhabiting the garden, many of them predators on the so-called pests, especially those which feed on vegetables. If you like particular kinds of plants and specialize in, say, a tremendous show of dahlias, or beds full of roses, leaving little room for anything else to grow, you will not only decrease the types of insects, but you will also provide a feast for the pests which prey on dahlias or roses. There will not be enough predators to deal with them, because of the shortage of other kinds of plants; moreover, they will spread to the other plants, including vegetables and fruit, as they breed and reproduce unchecked and run out of suitable food. Greenfly, earwigs, capsid bugs and blackfly are a few examples of problems which can build up in these circumstances. Diseases, too, such as mildew and grey mould, can become epidemic.

But with a great diversity of plants and the insects that come with them, which of course will include bees and butterflies, will come more and varied birds, bats and small mammals – hedgehogs, voles, field mice, possibly a dormouse, though these are now so rare that they are an endangered species – and reptiles such as frogs and toads, grass snakes and the slow-worm, again disappearing breeds. The mixed-plant garden thus becomes a power-house for natural controls.

It will do no harm if there is a bed or border planted solely with your favourite plant, but that particular genus should not dominate the garden, unless you are prepared to sacrifice organic gardening. In any case, whatever the specialist plant is, in a mixed-plant garden it will grow all the better and benefit from the attention of the insects originally attracted by the alternative plants.

SPACING

The enthusiastic gardener will have no difficulty in filling the garden with a mixture of plants; the problem is much more likely to be that he or she needs a garden at least five times the size to grow just a few of all the plants that are coveted – a piece of ground covering a hundred acres would probably do nicely! But in the desire to cultivate as many species and varieties as possible, it is easy to cram them in, to see a space and fill it with a new plant which needs a metre or so (several feet) in which to spread and in fact only has about 45 cm (18 in). This is the way to disaster. Crowded plants unable to extend their shoots and branches naturally, become drawn and leggy, and the lack of light means that they are pale and weak. All this predisposes them to infestation by insects, while the crowded surroundings ensure a humid atmosphere and little air circulation, enabling fungus diseases to spread rapidly as well.

It is important to try to give your plants headroom. After all, there is no pleasure in watching them slowly die an unpleasant death, especially when they could have been thriving and beautiful with a little more thought on your part. Garden centres, nurseries, plant catalogues, all will give brief information on a plant's size as well as its needs and appearance, so that you can determine the area it requires in advance of planting.

PLANTS FOR PLACES

Another point which is easy to overlook once you are bitten with the gardening bug is the need to put a plant in a place which naturally suits it, and indeed, doing so is at least half the battle in making a success of organic gardening. One of the most basic needs of certain plants is for an acid soil; all the ericaceous (heather) family plants must have this kind of soil – rhododendrons, azaleas, the heaths and heathers themselves, *Pieris formosa forrestii* (flame of the forest) and vaccinium are some of them. If you plant them in an alkaline soil, they will turn yellow and die fairly quickly unless you water them frequently with an expensive solution of nutrients of a special kind; even so they will never really thrive.

It helps in deciding what plants to grow where if you can look at your garden, and determine what kind of habitats it has in it. There are bound to be shady areas, sunny hot ones, places which are windy and so on. In one part the soil may always be rather wet, in another it could easily be acid, next to an alkaline patch, and somewhere else perennial drying out may be its characteristic. Each of these will dictate the type of plant to grow in them, and if you fit the plant to the place like this, there is a much greater chance that they will live long and healthy lives.

SOIL

As with any other type of plant in the garden, keeping the soil in good condition with the regular addition of humus derived from rotted organic matter is a further vital necessity, together with feeding in the form of an organic fertilizer such as blood-fish-and-bone or organic Growmore. Some plants will grow well in a soil which does not contain much mineral plant nutrient, because that is part of the habitat from which they originate. Many Mediterranean plants will thrive in such a soil provided it drains well and the site is a sun-trap. But the majority of plants grown in temperate-climate gardens will need a mixture of about 14 or 15 minerals always available in the soil, the consequences of which will be plants with strong stems that are not always flopping over and needing supports, richly coloured, plentiful flowers and, in addition to these benefits, more than enough new growth every year on the perennial varieties. More details on soil care will be found in Chapter 3.

GENERAL CARE

Besides starting the plants in the right way, there will certainly be some ongoing care needed once they are established. The hard physical work comes with the preparation and planting; after that the chores are much easier. For instance, dead-heading, which is one of them, only needs a pair of secateurs, sometimes not even those, but it is an important job, as it encourages the plants to produce more flowers. However, no great harm is done if you leave them on, and this can in fact do good, as the seedheads will attract more and different birds, and any seeds that germinate may produce some delightful new varieties.

Annuals which have finished flowering will need to be dispatched to the compost heap, and their place filled at once, to prevent a weed take-over. Bulbs should be left to die down naturally, even if the leaves do look untidy. The bulb manufactures food with the help of leaves for the next season's flowers, and cutting them off while still green could easily ensure no display the following season. If you really cannot bear the sight of bulb leaves lying all over the bed, tie them in a knot, but even that can cause trouble.

PRUNING

Shrubs and climbing plants will all need pruning at intervals as the spring and summer go on. Mostly it is a matter of removing growth which has flowered so that the new shoots are allowed a share of air and light; sometimes, to stimulate new growth, the oldest shoots or branches have to be cut right off, back to their point of origin. Climbers tend to get very tangled, and need regular controlling if they are to be seen at their best, especially clematis.

As a good rule-of-thumb, prune any shrub or climber immediately after flowering if it flowers between spring and early summer. If it flowers after that, prune the following spring when the parts that have been killed by winter cold can also be removed. Always cut back to just above a bud or leaf or strong new shoot. Clematis which flower in mid to late summer should be cut down in early spring to about 60 cm (2 ft) to provide the best flowering display each year. Wisteria needs summer and winter pruning; the new shoots are cut to six leaves in late summer, and then to one or two buds in winter. Virginia creeper and honeysuckle can be left to their own devices.

Whatever else you do or don't do to prune a plant, always remove dead growth completely – the bark will be brown, and probably peeling or flaking off, and the wood will snap cleanly. Another general help is to remove weak shoots and also shoots or branches where there are many crowded together, thinning them out so that the remainder can get a share of air and light. The best time to do this is spring, just as new growth is starting to appear.

UNDER-GLASS GARDENING

For those of you that garden under glass, whether it is a greenhouse or conservatory, the main problem lies in avoiding the use of chemicals to control pests and diseases. As far as the growing medium is concerned, special composts are always used for plants in containers, either soilless, containing peat, sand and fertilizers, or soil-containing, such as the John Innes type whose ingredients are exactly the same, but with the addition of good loam and chalk (there is also a J.I. compost without chalk, for acid-soil plants). From the organic viewpoint, these are not too bad; the problem is the fertilizer, which is all or partially artificial. You can make up your own composts, however, using an organic fertilizer in the form of organic Growmore.

A soilless compost consists of granulated peat and fine silver sand in the ratio 3:1, to which organic Growmore can be added at the rate recommended by the makers, together with 28 g (1 oz) chalk per bushel; a soil-containing John Innes type potting compost consists of 7 parts good loam, 3 parts granulated peat and 2 parts coarse sand, plus organic Growmore, and 21 g ($\frac{3}{4}$ oz) chalk per bushel. However, with experience, it is possible to modify the proportions and to use different ingredients suited to particular types of plants. Fine leafmould used to be essential in potting composts; you can also use composted conifer bark or sieved garden compost to take the place of some of the peat and/or soil.

Pest and disease control in these confined conditions can be difficult as the warmth, moisture and lack of natural predators are ideal for their continued existence and reproduction. But a two-pronged attack can be made on them: one is by introducing natural predators and parasites, details of which are given on pp. 80–89, combined with the use of natural sprays, and the other is preventing them from appearing at all by your treatment of the plants.

POSITION FOR PLANTS

As with any outside plant, giving them the right environment to start with, and then supplying what they need from day to day, is about four-fifths of the battle to keep pests and fungal diseases at bay. Always be sure that, when you introduce a new plant, it is not already infested with some unpleasant alien; keep it in quarantine separately from other plants for a few weeks if you are at all uneasy about its health. Choose your plants for the conditions of the greenhouse or conservatory; for instance trying to grow a nephrolepis fern in a south-facing conservatory will only result in yellow fronds and an infestation of scale insect; it needs shade, cool temperatures and a moist atmosphere. You would do better to specialize in cacti in such a situation, and should have some beautiful flowering specimens as a result.

TEMPERATURES

Once the right plants are in the right place, their daily care will involve the manipulation of temperature, humidity and ventilation, together with applications of water and food. The majority of plants under glass are there because they are tropical or semi tropical, so summer temperatures can be allowed to rise naturally to about 32°C (90°F), or higher. But with these really high temperatures, plenty of humidity is important, provided by frequent overhead misting with clear water and trays or pot saucers of water near the plants to provide water vapour through evaporation. In winter, a minimum temperature of 7°C (45°F) is acceptable in most cases, especially if the compost is not watered very much, so that it is on the dry side all the time. Plants can survive cold much better if their roots are not wet and standing in soggy compost.

When the weather is hot, plenty of ventilation is essential, with top and side ventilators open, and a door as well. If top ventilation is not possible, as can be the case with conservatories, open all the doors on really hot days, and get a through draught. Aim for a steady temperature, and keep it in the range 21–30°C (70–85°F) in summer. Watering is extremely important at this time if plants have thin leaves, as they transpire water vapour so fast through them that twice daily watering can be necessary. Always give enough, at each watering, to fill the space at the top of the container between the compost surface and the rim and repeat if no surplus drains through into the pot saucer; if there is still a surplus after 20 minutes or so, throw it away. Plants with thick leaves store water in them, and will live with much less moisture than their thin-leaved neighbours. If these varieties are given too much before the compost becomes dry on the surface, the roots rot. If in doubt about when to water, lift the container. A lightweight one will be ready for moisture, and the compost surface, as well as being dry, will be light coloured.

NUTRIENTS

Feeding during the growing season depends on the species of plant. Some of them grow fast and rapidly absorb the nutrients in the compost, others do not need any extra until repotted the following spring, when the new compost will contain the necessary food. If feeding is necessary, either new compost and a bigger pot can be given, or liquid feeds once a week can be applied, such as the seaweed fertilizer 'Maxicrop', or other organically-based solutions. Signs of the need for feed are a sudden slowing down of growth, paling of the green of the leaves, and dwindling of flower production. Liquid feeding is convenient as it does two jobs at once, and it is easy for the roots to take up the nutrients and make good the deficiency quickly.

CHAPTER 10

PEST AND DISEASE MANAGEMENT

The treatment of plant pests and diseases is the biggest bone of contention between organic and non-organic gardeners, and causes more discussion than any other aspect. But before you start considering how to get rid of the organisms living on your plants, ask yourself how bad are they really? Certainly, if you are losing entire crops, something has to be done about it, but not necessarily in the form of sprays or powders to destroy the organism.

As a start, for future reference it would be worth going back to the beginning, to determine whether the soil conditions were right for the plants, and then deciding whether the subsequent care was also right. Even unseasonal weather can usually be mitigated to some extent.

But if you have only the occasional greenfly, the odd bit of mildew on a few plants, or one or two strawberries rotting with grey mould, spraying the whole lot could be an unnecessary overkill. Leaf spots are a case in point. Many, many plants have spotting on their foliage at some time in their lives, variously coloured brown, grey, yellow or black, of various sizes, and produced by a variety of causes. Sun scorch, minor fungus diseases, hail and poor soil drainage are some of them, and many gardeners worry about them quite unnecessarily. You need only be concerned if the spotting is spreading steadily and the plants are losing their normal colouring and slowing down production of new growth, whether it is flowers, shoots or fruit.

The message is: learn to live with some degree of plague, but keep an eye on it (observation is one of the key words in good gardening).

Provided you carry out the principles and ideas outlined in the earlier chapters, particularly those in Chapter 3, much of the work in controlling pests and diseases will be done for you by your garden helpers, mostly insects and small mammals. Occasionally there are epidemics, and these should really be the only time when chemical controls are necessary; fortunately there are some natural chemicals to use which do little or no harm to the rest of the garden. Before you resort to these, however, give your helpers a chance to earn their keep. For instance, when the weather is hot and dry in early summer, greenfly tend to multiply astronomically but a population of hoverflies will decimate them.

BENEFICIAL INSECTS

Ladybirds are among the most useful of insects as they and their larvae – small, black, crocodile-like creatures about 6 mm ($\frac{1}{4}$ in) long – predate aphids, thrips, mites, scale insects and mealy bugs. Adult ladybirds hibernate in winter and lay eggs from spring until well into summer. The larvae which hatch from these live for about three weeks before they pupate, and the new adult emerges well before the end of summer.

Hoverflies are also of great use. Their larvae are the main parasites of aphids, and it is not unusual for them to destroy aphids at the rate of one a minute. The commonly noticed hoverflies are striped black and yellow so that they look like wasps, but they have fatter bodies, and hover above flowers. They are especially attached to *Limnanthes douglasii* (bacon and egg flower), a pretty little annual with yellow and white saucer-shaped flowers, which is easily grown in sun or shade and moist soil. Adult hoverflies lay eggs close to aphid infestations, and the larvae which hatch from them are pale and about 6 mm ($\frac{1}{4}$ in) long. They feed and then pupate over the course of about two weeks, after which adults emerge and the cycle starts again. Many generations can therefore be produced in one season.

Lacewings of various species, including a pretty flying kind with pale green transparent wings, capsid and shield bugs, other flies and ground beetles, are more insects which help to decimate populations of thrips, aphids, caterpillars, red spider mites and other pests. Ground beetles, as well as attacking a variety of insects, will devour small slugs, and parasitic wasps are particularly attracted to caterpillars.

The population of insects in an unsprayed garden is immense and, if left to themselves, jungle warfare is undoubtedly the order of the day, but it does save you practically all the trouble of spraying.

SMALL MAMMALS

Hedgehogs have always had a good press, and are even more popular now as moppers-up of slugs and snails, doing their good work at night. You can encourage their presence in the garden by providing an undisturbed shelter: a heap of prunings or leaves which you can do without, under which they can spend the winter, and a saucer of milk at night (tinned cat food is said to be acceptable, too!).

Frogs and toads are slug eaters, and will in fact eat other small living creatures as well. A pool in the garden is bound to attract them, especially as most of the natural water reservoirs have disappeared, due to farm and building drainage schemes. Birds are great insect eaters, and you will attract a great variety of species with the right choice of plants.

You may have unwanted small mammals such as mice, which are partial to fruit, seeds, bulbs and bark, but they are less likely to eat these if there is plenty of other food, as there will be in the organic garden.

MECHANICAL CONTROLS

Also useful in the organic treatment of plant diseases and pests, which also avoid the use of chemicals, are various physical and mechanical methods. One of the best is removal of pests by hand, either using finger and thumb to mash a heavy infestation of aphids, or to pick off caterpillars and maggots. Wholesale removal of shoots, leaves, flowers and even plants which are badly attacked by aphids of various kinds, or any tiny, slow-moving insect, is the most effective and quickest way of dealing with such outbreaks.

Traps can be used, for instance baited foods which are attractive to pests, sticky papers or papers impregnated with attractants. Scarers of various kinds will keep birds off crops, seeds and newly sown lawns; unpleasant smelling but harmless deterrents are useful against cats, dogs, squirrels, deer, rabbits, birds, mice and voles, and moles. Protectants which physically cover the plants with some form of material, are other harmless aids preventing damage, especially useful where crops are concerned, as they are not necessarily ornamental. Netting, mini greenhouses, black plastic and cardboard shields are some of them.

ORGANIC CHEMICAL CONTROLS

Lastly, if good husbandry, garden helpers and mechanical methods have still not overcome a particular problem, safe chemical controls can be tried which do not harm the environment, do not persist, and some of which only kill the pest or disease concerned. If you are forced to use any of these, remember that you may be killing predators and parasites as well, and that you will be taking a link out of the food chain, thus upsetting the garden balance, however safe the chemical. It will take time to restore this, and in the meanwhile some other trouble may be building up – in other words the side-effects can be more troublesome than the cure.

Organic chemicals to use include the following:

BORDEAUX MIXTURE
A fungicide which is especially useful for preventing blight from infecting potatoes and tomatoes, but also helps control mildew, rust and a variety of leaf spot diseases.

BURGUNDY MIXTURE

Also a fungicide, containing washing soda instead of quicklime. Stronger than Bordeaux Mixture and liable therefore to be more damaging, it is nevertheless particularly useful in dealing with rust fungus diseases.

DERRIS

A vegetable insecticide made from the ground-up tuberous root of *Derris elliptica*, a climbing evergreen member of the pea family from tropical Asia, where it is used as a fish poison. It is good for controlling caterpillars and aphids, ants and earwigs, also red spider mite to some degree, and is harmless to bees. The active part of it is rotenone, and the efficiency of derris depends on the quality of this present in the product and its age. Different dilution rates are recommended by the suppliers, according to the pests to be controlled. It is a contact poison, so the solution must touch the insect's body. A good drenching spray is required.

PYRETHRUM

Another vegetable insecticide, this time made from flowers taken from *Chrysanthemum cinerarifolium*, grown for the purpose in East Africa. It has a quick 'knockdown' effect, and is particularly good for controlling various aphids. Ants, weevils and flea beetles, sawfly caterpillars and leaf-hoppers are other pests affected. As with derris, the insect must come into contact with it, so a plant has to be well sprayed, and combining the two is the best way of using them.

Associated with pyrethrum there is a group of new chemicals produced as a result of recent research for new and safe pesticides. One of these is permethrin, an analogue of pyrethrum which is extremely similar to it in chemical composition, but which is in fact safer and more effective. It lasts longer than pyrethrum, which can quite soon lose its efficacy under the effects of air and sunlight. Both pyrethrum and permethrin are non-toxic to warm-blooded animals, but dangerous to fish.

QUASSIA

A solution of this is extremely bitter to taste, and it is one of the substances used as a deterrent against small and large mammals. Quassia is made from chips of the wood of *Picrasma excelsa*, a tropical tree from the Far East. Use it as a drenching spray. It is useful against aphids and small caterpillars such as newly hatched sawfly larvae on gooseberries.

SOFT SOAP

Much used as a spreader for other insecticides, so that the solution runs all over the leaf or stem instead of remaining as separate droplets, soft soap is an insecticide in its own right, chiefly useful for aphid and caterpillar control.

SULPHUR

A fungicide which was once much used for powdery mildew control, flowers of sulphur have never lost their efficacy, and can be applied as a dust or a spray. Sulphur will also control black spot on roses and scab on top fruit. Although a fungicide, it has some insecticidal use and, unfortunately, on some predatory and parasitic species of insect as well. A further complication is that it can burn the leaves of redcurrants and some varieties of apples – follow makers' directions in this respect. The warning about applying any chemical, even organic, and upsetting the garden's balance, is particularly applicable here.

Besides these, there are further remedies, not always chemical nor applied as sprays or dusts, but as they are very specific, they will be described under the particular problems to which they relate.

UNIVERSAL PESTS AND DISEASES

There are vast numbers of pests and diseases which infect plants and which are, as has been seen, themselves infected by others or preyed upon by larger creatures such as hedgehogs and birds. Among these are some which are common to all plants, in the same way that colds are universal to human beings. The following list describes these insects, mammals and fungi, and bacteria, and details appropriate remedies.

ANTS

Need no description; there are black ants and so-called red ants. Though regarded as plant pests, they do not actually feed on plants but act as 'nurses' to greenfly in order to acquire the sweet secretions produced by these and other aphids. They are often seen running up and down stems and leaves on which there are aphid colonies.

Where they can cause trouble is in the production of nests (ant-hills) beneath plants, especially shrubs and small trees, as the fine roots are often left dangling in the air of their tunnels. As ant-hills tend to consist of fine dry soil, the plant suffers from lack of water. Dowsing them with cold water discourages them; boiling water will kill them, or use derris. Make a hole in the ant-hill and pour the solution down it.

APHIDS

Sometimes called plant lice, an apt description when you see the tips of stems and leaves literally crawling with the tiny green insects. There are other types: blackfly are aphids, and there are grey, blue-grey, and pink aphids, as well as less common species in yet more colours. They suck the sap from plants through needle-like mouthparts, and cause most trouble between spring and the end of early summer. though they can easily be present for the rest of the summer as well.

Be prepared for infestations in dry hot weather in particular. Round about midsummer many develop wings and fly off to different host plants on which to lay eggs, while others remain on the same plant. One aphid can mature within a week, and then produce living young asexually at such a speed that literally tons of aphids could theoretically be produced in three months from one individual. Fortunately, natural controls can prevent this.

The damage aphids do mainly consists of stunting, discolouring and distorting growth, weakening a plant considerably in heavy attacks. In addition, they are carriers of virus diseases in the plant's sap as they move from infected to healthy plants. There is no cure for viruses, and eventually they can be lethal.

Weak plants are more badly infected with aphids, so always keep plants growing well. Use finger and thumb to remove minor infestations and be very watchful; completely remove heavily attacked shoots and leaves. Use sprays or dusts of soft soap, derris, pyrethrum (permethrin) or quassia.

BIRDS

In large Victorian walled gardens, cats were encouraged to roam about, or were even kept tethered in them; they are still useful bird scarers! Other deterrents are proprietary brands of unpleasant smelling substances, such as quassia, anthraquinone and naphthalene. There are also bird-scarers such as glitterbangs, hum-lines, scarecrows, and protectants of netting, black cotton or brushwood, used to protect seed-beds, ripening fruit and fruiting vegetables, and a rayon webbing (Scaraweb) for fruit and flowering trees and bushes, which is biodegradable.

Birds chiefly cause damage by scuffling up seed-beds (sparrows), pecking fruit and fruiting vegetables (blackbirds and others), tearing off fruiting and flowering buds (bullfinches) – do not prune gooseberries until early spring – and eating brassicas in winter (pigeons).

CAPSIDS

These bugs are large, sap-sucking insects with a body about 6 mm ($\frac{1}{4}$ in) long; they run quickly over the foliage and soil. They feed on young leaves and shoot tips, producing pinholes in them which coalesce so that the leaves become ragged and growth is severely checked. Present from late spring–midsummer. Blackcurrants, gooseberries, apples, pears, plums, strawberries, chrysanthemums, fuchsias, hydrangeas, potatoes, are particularly prone to infestation. Difficult to control as it moves down to soil level as soon as disturbed, and escapes: keep weeds under control so that it has nowhere to hide and spray or dust derris, which must touch it to be effective.

CATERPILLARS AND MAGGOTS
These eat holes in leaves, stems, flowers, fruits and, if soil-living, roots as well. Notorious caterpillars are those of the cabbage-white butterfly (Fig. 13), gooseberry sawfly, winter moth, apple sawfly and the crane-fly. The last-named produces the larvae commonly known as leatherjackets: grey-brown caterpillars which live in the soil and feed on the roots of lawn-grasses, young plants and seedlings. Remove by hand on sight; spray derris, or derris and pyrethrum combined or Bactospeine, a proprietary bacterial control especially useful for cabbage caterpillars. Dig or fork soil thoroughly in autumn and spring to expose overwintering caterpillars and chrysalids to birds and to frost and snow.

GREY MOULD (BOTRYTIS CINEREA)
A fungus disease characterized by grey fur above yellow spotting or patching of leaves, and grey fur on flowers, stems and fruits, the part beneath becoming rotten and discoloured. Spreads rapidly in confined, cool and moist conditions, and can be particularly bad in cool summers and on plants under glass. Remove affected parts as soon as seen and place on compost heap; use protective spray, such as sulphur or Bordeaux Mixture, on rest of plant.

MICE, MOLES, SQUIRRELS, RABBITS, DEER
All except squirrels will eat and strip bark off trees and shrubs in winter; mice are partial to fruit, seeds and bulbs; squirrels will take unripe strawberries, nuts and seeds; rabbits will eat most young vegetables; deer will eat young shoots.

Repellents which smell unpleasant to the animal concerned, without being harmful, are the best way of preventing damage when using chemicals. Tree guards in the form of plastic collars will prevent removal of bark, as will cylinders of wire netting, and should be put in place at planting time. Netting will protect vegetables and soft fruit, but it must be well secured all the way round as squirrels, in particular, are notorious for finding a way in. To prevent deer damage, the only certain way is to put 1.8 m (6 ft) wire in place to keep them out. Moles dislike strong smells – Jeyes fluid in their runs will help – also prickly leaves such as holly.

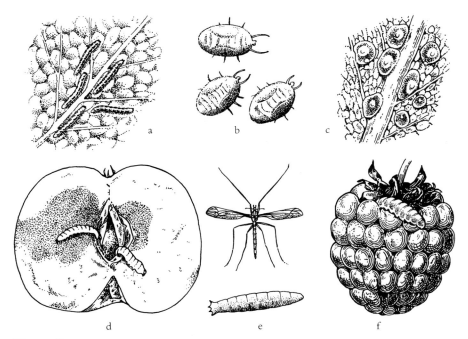

Fig. 13 Pests
(*a*) Caterpillars of cabbage white butterflies; handpick or use a parasitic spray.
(*b*) Juvenile forms of whitefly as scales on the underside of a leaf. (*c*) Scale insects clustered along the main vein on the underside of a leaf. (*d*) Larvae of the codling moth enters an apple through the 'eye' and penetrates to the centre where it eats the pips. (*e*) The cranefly or daddy-long-legs is the adult of the soil-living grub called a leatherjacket, which feeds on grass and small-plant roots. (*f*) The small white grub-like larvae of the raspberry beetle feed on the ripening fruits.

MILDEW, POWDERY
A fungal disease which forms white patches on the surface of leaves, stems, fruit and occasionally flowers, which may also become discoloured. It weakens and stunts growth, results in bud-dropping, and causes rotting of fruit in due course. Worst attacks in late summer, particularly if soil is dry and there is much humidity. Remove infected growth immediately; on apples and roses cut back to healthy growth, then spray or dust with sulphur.

RED SPIDER MITE
A minute pest which lives on the underside of leaves, sucking sap from them. Difficult to see without a magnifying lens. Colour can be red, pink or yellowish, cast skins are white, and eggs transparent. They are not the comparatively large velvety red mites seen without a lens: these are not damaging to plants, and in fact help to keep woolly aphid (see fruit pests) under control.

Attacked leaves become greyish or yellowish speckled on dull green, and eventually wither and fall. Plant will look as though short of water, and growth will cease. Webbing can also be produced.

These mites cause more trouble in hot dry environments, so keeping plants well watered and in a moist but well ventilated atmosphere prevents attacks in the first place. If present outdoors, spray thoroughly with derris. Fortunately, in the unsprayed garden these mites should not be a pest as they have many natural predators. In greenhouses and conservatories, introduce the predatory mite *Phytoseiulus persimilis* (proprietary name Spidex), and follow maker's instructions.

RUST
A fungal disease which takes the form of red-brown or yellow-brown raised small spots on the surface of leaves, causing early falling, weakening of the plant, and poor flowering. Can be a particular problem on hollyhocks, roses, gooseberries, mints, antirrhinums and sweet willams. Removing by hand and burning the infected leaves should be followed by spraying with Bordeaux or Burgundy Mixture.

SLUGS AND SNAILS
These eat large holes in leaves near soil level, but also higher up from stems and flowers, and will feed on bulbs and tubers, and fruiting vegetables and fruits close to the soil. Feeding is at night, resting is in daytime under stones and containers or in suitably dark nooks and crannies.

Collect troublesome slugs and snails after dark by torchlight, and drown or remove to distant fields and woods; trap under pieces of tile or slate placed amongst plants/crops; attract with potato peelings, citrus halves or saucers of stale beer; encourage helpers such as ground beetles by providing them with slates, etc. as protection, and frogs and hedgehogs (see pp. 12 and 11), and thrushes (see p. 11). As a last resort use tapes impregnated with metaldehyde, or pads beneath potatoes when planting, though as worms pull the ends down into the soil, there may be some contamination of the soil in due course. Water the soil with a solution of aluminium sulphate (available in several proprietary forms) to control eggs, young and young adults, but remember that it must actually come into contact with the slugs or snails.

WHITEFLY
Tiny winged insect pests which look like white moths, cluster on underside of leaves. Young are minute round transparent 'scales' which suck the sap from the leaves; these become very sticky, messy and distorted, with sooty mould growing on them, and growth ceases. Especially

troublesome on cabbages; destroy badly infested plants, spray remainder with pyrethrum (permethrin) or soft soap solution to kill the scales. Do not leave stumps of cabbage family plants which are no longer cropping in the soil. Whitefly can also be serious on fuchsias, tomatoes, chrysanthemums, cineraria, primula and pelargonium (geranium). Under glass use parasitic wasp *Encarsia formosa* (Enstrip) as suppliers direct; note that it is not effective on outdoor cabbage whitefly.

WOODLICE
Insects with a grey, hard-plated covering which roll up into a ball for protection. These do not cause a great deal of damage unless there is no decaying vegetation for them to feed on, but can then attack roots of container-grown plants at the drainage holes, seedlings in open ground, and stems of young plants at soil level. Will also be found in great quantities in certain types of compost heaps, i.e. those which are dry, and also in undisturbed conditions. Cultivate and generally disturb areas where they collect, re-structure the compost heap and moisten it, and use boiling water to kill them if they still do not disperse.

SPECIFIC PESTS AND DISEASES

Besides these ubiquitous troubles, there are others which are specific to particular plant species, types of plant, or conditions. Some are extremely serious as regards the damage they can do and the speed with which they can spread. The most troublesome of these are described in the following list.

ORNAMENTALS
Rose black spot A fungus disease mainly of the leaves; symptoms are black fringed spots and blotches; leaves yellow and fall prematurely; bush may be completely defoliated by midsummer. Grow resistant varieties; do not plant in a very hot sunny site – a little occasional shade is good for roses during the day. Collect infected leaves and shoots, and either burn or bury them deeply in the soil beneath the roses, and mulch thickly in late winter or early spring. If infected leaves hang on late into winter, pick off before spring.

Leafminer An insect pest which is the larva of a fly. The tiny maggot burrows into leaf surfaces and produces winding pale coloured lines or tunnels, or else large, pale brown blisters. In bad infestations whole leaf is mined and most of them damaged. Plants particularly attacked are chrysanthemums, holly, laburnum, lilac, and under glass, cinerarias and primulas. Remove and destroy affected leaves or bury them deeply in the soil. Not very responsive to organic sprays, but in any case it is difficult to spray a fully-grown holly!

PLANTS UNDER GLASS

Mealy bug   A sap-sucking insect which remains in one place all its life while feeding, and covers itself with white protective fluff; most serious on bulbs where it feeds between bases of leaves, making it difficult to reach. Pick off by hand as thoroughly as possible; use a soft brush and methylated or surgical spirit dabbed on to the fluff so as to penetrate it.

Scale insect   Another sap-sucking insect, which remains stationary, like mealy bug, but has a hard brown, grey or black shell; size is about 3 mm ($\frac{1}{8}$ in) long, young are much smaller and pale green. Found on underside of leaves and on bark of leaf stalks, stems and trunks. Serious on ferns, citrus, bay tree, palms, camellia, rubber plant (ficus species), stephanotis, but also infests many other plants. Remove by hand using finger nails, as soon as seen, and isolate infested plant at once; spray with soft soap.

Sooty mould   A fungus which produces black, soot-like patches on leaf upper surfaces. These actually grow on the honeydew secreted by sap-sucking insects, and do not harm the leaf beyond blocking the breathing pores. Sponge off gently with warm, clean water.

VEGETABLES

Broad bean chocolate spot   Fungus producing dark brown blotches and spots on leaves and stems of plants, which spread rapidly in dull, damp cool seasons and can destroy crop. Grow plants well spaced out, in sun and well-drained soil. Destroy worst affected plants as soon as seen, and spray remainder with Bordeaux Mixture.

Carrot (and onion) fly   Tiny white maggots burrow into root or bulb and feed on it; secondary rotting often follows. Eggs laid in surface soil close to plants in early summer and again in late summer. Flies are attracted by smell of bruised foliage so thin affected plants during evening, or sow thinly enough to avoid need for spacing out later. If there are any thinnings, bury them deeply in the compost heap. Keep soil close to plants well hoed once they germinate; mask smell with parsley or garlic grown near by. Use onion sets, as these are never attacked.

Cabbage root fly   Maggots burrow into main root, and top growth becomes dull, dark grey coloured, wilts and collapses. Young plants

Slugs feed mainly on leaves but will also eat flowers and buds: this black garden slug is feeding on a tulip.

mainly attacked by successive broods all through summer. All cabbage family vulnerable, including wallflowers. Prevent infestation with cardboard or polystyrene foam sheets, make collars out of them by cutting squares with a central hole and a slit from outer edge to the hole, then fit round the plant stem on the soil surface. Dig soil well in autumn to expose overwintering pupae to birds.

Parsnip canker　Dark brown or black markings on shoulders of root, followed by rotting. Use resistant varieties, keep soil well supplied with lime and well-drained, and do not sow until mid–late spring.

Pea maggot　Tiny green larvae which feed on peas in pods; hatch from eggs laid by moths on the embryo pods, just as the flower falls. Spray with soft soap about a week after flowering starts. Alternatively, sow at the end of early summer to avoid main brood, or grow mangetout, which are not attacked. Dig ground in autumn to expose overwintering cocoons to birds.

Potato blackleg Unusual since it is a bacterial disease. Leaves turn yellow and wither, base of stem blackens and top growth collapses; tuber rots where stem is attached to it. Lift and destroy complete plant; do not leave any tubers in the soil. In future examine seed tubers carefully before planting for any signs of softening or rotting. The disease is not retained in the soil, only on the tubers, hence the need to destroy them.

Potato blight (also in tomato) Leaves develop brown-black blotches which spread to the stems and down into the tubers. All top growth rots and collapses, and tubers also have brown markings, and rot. Expect infections in warm, wet summers. Spray with Bordeaux Mixture once a fortnight from the beginning of midsummer, to cover the leaves with a protective fungicide. Grow resistant varieties such as 'Home Guard', 'Stormont Enterprise' and 'Maris Peer', which will resist most, though not all, of the strains of this fungus disease. Burn the infected haulm and tubers, making sure that every single tuber is removed from the soil.

Potato scab A fungus producing dark, rough patches on the tuber skin. There are quite a few more or less resistant varieties, for example, 'Pentland Javelin', 'Maris Peer', and 'Pentland Crown'. Scab is worse on alkaline soils, so do not lime in advance; use lawn mowings, peat or leafmould to line the planting holes. Do not plant seed tubers which are already scabbed.

Tomato wilt (sleepy disease) A soil-living fungus disease which infects plants through the roots and is worst on soil lacking humus, or where tomatoes are grown repeatedly. Leaves wilt in hot sun at midday, then recover, lower leaves turn yellow and later wilting becomes permanent. Centre of stem at base has brown staining, shown when stem is cut across.

Improve health of plants by mulching with peat or potting compost close to stem to encourage production of new roots into sterile growing medium, spray plants overhead daily and raise the temperature, if possible, where plants are growing under glass. Take off what crop can be saved, then destroy the plants including the root, and grow tomatoes elsewhere for two or three years, or use plants grafted on to wilt-resistant stock.

FRUIT
Brown rot A fungus disease mainly affecting the fruit, which produces brown rotting of the fruit on the tree, on which there are concentric rings of white pustules. Plums, gages, apples and pears mainly affected, but also

cherries and peaches. Infected fruits can be mummified on the tree; fruit spurs and flower buds can be killed by the fungus. Destroy infected parts as soon as seen, prune to remove cankered shoots in winter, destroy rotting fruits in store, and do not store bruised or damaged fruit.

Codling moth   Small dirty white caterpillars with brown heads enter apples through 'eye' of fruit and bore into centre where they eat pips, then leave fruit and pupate in soil. Infected fruit remains small, colours prematurely and falls to ground; maggots present in mid and late summer. Use proprietary traps for male moths hung in trees; sacking bands round tree trunks help as caterpillars form cocoons in them.

Mildew, American gooseberry   White patches on fruit, leaves and stems, likely to appear any time between spring and autumn, turning to brown, felt-like growth which eventually rots berries and stunts growth. Cut out and destroy affected parts as soon as seen; use solution of sulphur twice, if variety not sulphur-shy, as soon as flowers have fallen and again three weeks later. Repeat if necessary at same intervals through season. Prune plants harder to improve air circulation between them and let in light, and improve soil drainage.

Raspberry beetle   White maggots eat ripening fruit; brownish small beetles attack the flowers. Can occur on other cane fruits. Spray derris as the flowers start to fall and repeat 10 days later when the berries are beginning to colour.

Scab   On apples and pears, black spots and patches on leaves and fruit, which then cracks where infected; stems of young shoots blister and eventually canker (bark cracks and shoot dies above canker). Worse in cool, wet springs and summers. Prune off all affected shoots in winter; destroy fallen infected leaves and fruits in summer/autumn. Spray every two weeks with sulphur from time leaves unfold. If sulphur-shy, use Bordeaux Mixture, also carefully.

Woolly aphid   An aphid which covers itself with white protective wool, and feeds on young stems and branches, particularly at forks. Worse in summer. Cut out badly affected stems and spray remainder with derris and soft soap under strong pressure.

Wasps   Usually feed on fruit which is already injured. If really bad, attract with jars of sweet water hung in trees; find and destroy nests with derris solution. Wasps can be predators of flies.

CHAPTER 11

ARE YOUR WEEDS REALLY NECESSARY?

People who don't know very much about gardening regard weeding as one of the main exercises, along with mowing the lawn and digging, so it is to be expected that gardening is considered both dull and hard work. Indeed, the removal of weeds is often thought to be the main job, a never-ending chore which one never quite gets on top of, particularly when dealing with pernicious brutes like bindweed and ground elder. It isn't surprising, therefore, that chemical sprays are often seen as a god-send, especially when they promise instant death, as paraquat does.

But one of the problems with chemical weedkillers is that they frequently kill seedlings from cultivated plants, which may be hybrids, in other words completely new plants with larger or differently coloured flowers to the parents, unusually coloured foliage, a different growth habit and so on, all desirable and all new. How many of these must have been destroyed in the last 20 or 30 years will never be known; perhaps now, by using modern versions of the old practices, they will not be lost, and an even greater variety of garden plants obtained.

I will not detail the drawbacks to using weedkillers but, briefly, some are poisonous to humans, others result in changes in soil structure. However careful one is, it is also difficult in many cases to avoid treating the cultivated plants as well as the weeds; and accidents can easily happen if watering-cans are not thoroughly cleaned after use. It is very much simpler and less hard on one's pocket to pursue organic methods of control. Such controls do not involve the use of chemicals at all, but consist of a variety of cultural practices.

However, before you declare war on your weeds, do you really need to get rid of all of them? Apart from destroying the appearance of flower beds and borders, rose gardens and rockeries, they compete with the cultivated plants for light, air, moisture and nutrients, and provide a base from which pests and fungal diseases can be spread. All these points weigh heavily against them. But annual weeds can also provide a light cover to the soil which keeps it moist in hot dry weather, and perennial weeds in particular can draw up and absorb nutrients from the soil which might otherwise remain there, so that when dispatched to the compost heap, these nutrients, in due course, go into circulation for the benefit of the whole garden.

There is also the fact that they help to break up the soil with their roots, and add fibre to it — some of the best loam is to be found under meadow pastures. Clover and all the plants in the same family, the pea family, will increase the nitrogen content by the action of their roots and the roots of some weeds are actually helpful in producing secretions which destroy soil pests or fungi. It pays to think twice before uprooting weeds as soon as they appear; they can be useful.

WEED CONTROL BY CULTIVATION

Weed recognition is a help in deciding what is an undesirable alien and should be removed, and the most difficult ones are the most well-known. But identification is not essential; it is more important to determine how they increase themselves. Some weeds are annuals, and die down in one growing year, but only after flowering and setting seed, and this is their chief method of spreading. If you can do nothing else, remove the flowerheads before they open, or before seed is set; 'one year's seed is seven years' weeds', as the saying goes, and this applies equally to perennial weeds which live from year to year.

This other type of weed spreads differently, mainly by vegetative methods. They may have runners above the ground with plantlets at intervals which root, or underground stems which look like roots but which have buds on them, sprouting to produce stems and leaves, or they may have wide-spreading and tenacious root systems which sprout afresh when broken. Some taprooted weeds, like dandelions, will also do this, and it is very easy to pull a dandelion out, but leave the lower part of the root behind which then sprouts all over again. Docks and dandelions go in for both methods, as they produce masses of seed, and dock is particularly pernicious as it can remain in the soil, capable of germinating, but dormant, for more than 50 years!

So when handweeding, be particularly careful to remove the whole of the weed's root system if it is large and/or tenacious. Use a hand fork, or a hand cultivator such as a garden claw, a daisy grubber or a weed-extractor, a tough tool with a pointed end and two hooks. An ordinary border fork or a spade may be necessary for the larger weeds. If you can, eradicate the weeds while they're still seedlings; the job is almost painless then, and you can hoe them off quickly and easily with a Dutch hoe or a draw hoe. For small weed plants and largish areas, use a five-pronged cultivator tool — it helps to break up the surface soil as well.

Where you have to clear a large area which has not been cultivated for a long time, consisting of brambles, nettles, long grass, small saplings and similar problems, remove the top growth with a Hayter scythe, use for compost, put a rotary cultivator over the soil, and expose the roots cut by the cultivator tines to hot sun and/or drying winds. Fallow the area through the summer to allow for germination of dormant weed seeds, and hoe them off or use the cultivator again.

Before rotavating, you can use a flame gun to burn off the remnants of the top growth and to destroy the weed seeds in the top 1.5 cm ($\frac{1}{2}$ in) of soil. This is also a useful method for large areas covered in annual weed growth.

WEED CONTROL BY MULCHING

Alternatively you can cover such an area in a mulch once it has been rotavated. Provided this is thick enough, it will suffocate the weeds, but it must prevent all light and air from reaching any top growth which may be appearing, so it needs not only to cover the area completely but should extend a foot or so beyond it.

Mulches are also useful around plants where the ground is clear of weeds already, but where there is no cover of cultivated plants. They will prevent the establishment of weeds in such situations, and so the soil some good at the same time, if they are organic.

WEED CONTROL BY GROUNDCOVER

The principle here is to prevent soil from remaining bare. If you remove a weed, fill the consequent space at once with a cultivated plant. If you leave it empty, some enterprising buttercup or plantain will make a take-over bid in no time. To cut down on the labour and time involved in constant planting, groundcover plants are ideal, and exhibit a good many of the characteristics of successful perennial weeds in that they grow rapidly and cover the soil. The difference is that they are ornamental and complement the plants they surround, and a good thick cover of such plants will defeat the majority of the weeds and prevent establishment.

Table 11.1 Some weeds on which butterfly caterpillars feed

Achillea millefolium – yarrow	*Rumex* species – dock
Alliaria petiolata – hedge garlic	*Taraxacum officinale* – dandelion
Arctium species – burdock	*Trifolium repens* – clover
Cirsium dissectum – meadow thistle	*Urtica dioica* – nettle
Malva – mallow	*Verbascum* – mullein

APPENDIX

SEEDSMEN

Atlas Organic Seeds, 10 Victoria Street, Braintree, Essex
J.W. Boyce, Bush Pasture, Lower Carter Street, Fordham, Ely, Cambs CB7 5RJ
Chase Organics (GB) Ltd., Addlestone, Weybridge, Surrey KT15 1HY
H.D.R.A. (Sales) Ltd., Ryton Gardens, Ryton-on-Dunsmore, Coventry CV8 3LG
Suffolk Herbs, Sawyers Farm, Little Cornard, Sudbury, Suffolk CO10 0NY
Suttons Seeds Ltd., Hele Road, Torquay, Devon TQ2 7QJ
Unwins Seeds Ltd., Impington Lane, Histon, Cambridge CB4 4LE

SUNDRIES SUPPLIERS

British Earthworm Technology, Harding Way, St Ives, Cambridge PE17 4WR
Bunting & Sons, Gt Horkesley, Colchester, Essex CO6 4AJ
Chase Organics (GB) Ltd., Addlestone, Weybridge, Surrey KT15 1HY
Chempak, Geddings Road, Hoddesdon, Herts EN11 0LR
Cornish Calcified Seaweed Ltd., Newham, Truro, Cornwall
Cowpact Products, P.O. Box 595, Adstock, Bucks MK18 2RE
Donaldson Paper & Board Sales Ltd., Suite 9, Essex House, 15 Station Road, Upminster, Essex RM14 2SJ
Gardiner's Organics, Brumley Brae, Elgin, Moray IV30 2PP (organic Growmore)
H.D.R.A. (Sales) Ltd., Ryton Gardens, Ryton-on-Dunsmore, Coventry CV8 3LG
Humber Fertilisers plc, P.O. Box 27, Stoneferry, Hull HU8 8DQ
Hydrocut Ltd., Sudbury, Suffolk CO10 6HB
Leggar Organics, Knapp Farm, Chads Hill, Cannington, Bridgwater, Somerset TA5 2BR
Impregnated Tapes Ltd., Lower Penarwyn, St Blazey, Par, Cornwall PL24 2DS

Maxicrop Ltd., 21 London Road, Gt Shelford, Cambridge CB2 5DF
Natural Pest Control, Watemead, Yapton Road, Barnham, Bognor
Regis, Sussex PO22 0BQ
Organic Concentrates Ltd., Little Chalfont, Amersham, Bucks HP5 4AP
Stimgro Ltd., Unit 2B, Longfield Road, Tunbridge Wells, Kent TN2
3EY
Synchemicals Ltd., Owen Street, Coalville, Leicester LE6 2DE (sulphur)
Vitaseamin (SC) Ltd., Woodside, Charney Road, Grange-over-Sands,
Cumbria

SOCIETIES AND ORGANIZATIONS

Biodynamic Agricultural Association, Emerson College, Forest Row,
London
Friends of the Earth, Mitcham, Surrey CR4 9AR
Good Gardeners' Association, Arkley Manor, Barnet, Herts
Greenpeace, 29–35 Gladstone Road, Croydon, Surrey
Henry Doubleday Research Association, Ryton Gardens, Ryton-on-
Dunsmore, Coventry CV8 3LG
National Institute for Agricultural Botany, Huntingdon Road, Cam-
bridge CB3 0LE
Organic Farmers & Growers Ltd., Abacus House, Station Road, Need-
ham Market, Ipswich, Suffolk IP6 8AT
Otley College of Agriculture & Horticulture, Otley, Ipswich, Suffolk
Soil Association Ltd., 86–88 Colston Street, Bristol BS1 5BB
Royal Horticultural Society, P.O. Box 313, Vincent Square, London
SW1P 2PE
Well Hall Country College, Well Alford, Lincs LN13 0ET
Working Weekends on Organic Farms (WWOOF), 19 Bradford Road,
Lewes, East Sussex BN7 5RB

BOOKS

The Backgarden Wildlife Sanctuary Book, R. Wilson, Penguin, 1977
Commonsense Compost-making, M.E. Bruce, Faber, reprinted 1975
Companion Planting, Gertrud Franck, Thorsons, 1983
Gardening for Butterflies, Madge Payne, British Butterfly Conservation
Society, 1987
Sanders Encyclopaedia of Gardening, Collingridge/Hamlyn, 1971 (rev. ed.)
Vegetables from Small Gardens, J. Larkcom, Faber, 1986 (rev. ed.)

In addition, a variety of publications is available from the H.D.R.A.
and there is an organic gardening magazine published from: Organic
Gardening, P.O. Box 4, Wivelscombe, Taunton, Somerset TA4 2QY.

INDEX